Walking With the Devil

WHAT PEOPLE ARE SAYING . . .

I've just finished reading a great book recently written and published by retired Minneapolis Police Officer Michael W. Quinn, a brutally frank expose of the "police code of silence" entitled *Walking With the Devil* (subtitled "What bad cops don't want you to know and good cops won't tell you"). Unlike so many police chiefs who like to gloss over the strong pressures and really difficult ethical dilemmas that result all too frequently in police officers. (Even the good ones) doing the wrong thing. Quinn exposes and unravels them, through a number of true stories, many of which the author participated in. Not only is the book a must read for anyone in law enforcement, but I believe it contains a lot of applicability to ethical dilemmas in all sorts of other professions and life situations.

Coleen Rowley, Retired FBI Agent,
Times Magazine 2002 Woman of the Year

Many people can never understand why a battered spouse doesn't just leave. I've written about that and understand it. But until I read *Walking With the Devil*, I never understood how a truly good cop could abide by, even embrace, the code of silence. I have written about the code's existence but never fully grasped how and why it exists. Mike Quinn has made a tremendous contribution with his "must read" exposition and explanation of this destructive phenomenon."

Kären M. Hess, B.S., M.S., M.A., PhD
Author of 30+ college text and trade books
Instructor and workshop facilitator

I just finished reading your book last night. It was fantastic, fantastic, fantastic and should be required reading for every officer. My compliments to you on having captured so perfectly the complexities of the issue of the Code of Silence. Take care and, again, my thanks for this outstanding book.

Kimberly Armstrong
Manager Professional Standards Branch
Edmonton Police Service, Canada

I firmly believe that Mike Quinn's book should be mandatory reading for all recruits attending a police academy and on the International Association of Chiefs of Police professional development reading list. Whenever the opportunity presents itself I give this as a gift to young people as they prepare to start their career in Law Enforcement.

Richard Thomas, Chief of Police, Port Washington, Wisconsin
and former Educational Consultant for the State of Wisconsin
Department of Justice, Training and Standards Bureau

Walking With the Devil examines the dynamics of "Code of Silence" and should be required reading for everyone embarking on a career in law enforcement. Mr. Quinn's insightful examination of this topic is engaging and dispels many of the myths surrounding the phenomenon of Code of Silence.

Sam Pettineo, Deputy Chief (Ret.), Evanston IL PD
Adjunct Instructor, Northwestern University's
Center for Public Safety

Michael W. Quinn is a retired Minneapolis Police Officer who is determined to bring to the attention of the public an informed and informative expose of what he calls the "police code of silence" in his book *Walking With the Devil: What bad cops don't want you to know and good cops won't tell you.* Deftly edited by Margot Willet, *Walking With the Devil* reveals why this police version of "Omerta" comes about and is enforced by the dangers of the job and the (sometimes misplaced) loyalties that arise from them. From training in a police academy, to the investigations of Internal Affairs, to scandal driven precinct shake ups, [Quinn] lays out everything in language and example that is accessible to the non-specialist general reader. Of special note is the section devoted to ten myths about policing which range from "street justice teaching people a lesson" to once being a part of a police "Code of Silence" you can't extricate yourself, to the necessity to be macho if you want to be effective in law enforcement. [Quinn] does more than just outline and document problems, he also offers advice for police administrators and line officers as to what can be done to weed out lawlessness from law enforcement. With the inclusion of a Glossary, References, and an Index, *Walking With the Devil* should be considered required reading for all police academia curriculums, and is highly recommended for anyone who is "on the job," as well as an essential reference for civilian review board members and concerned members of the community.

Midwest Book Review
Internet Bookwatch
Volume 15, No. 7, July 2005

I finally found the time to read your book, *Walking With the Devil: The Police Code of Silence.* I thoroughly enjoyed it and want to thank you again for sending me a copy. Your many accounts of your own career sparked a few flashbacks from my own. Although I did not work anywhere near as long as you did in street policing. I couldn't help reflect upon the truth of what you said: that the code of silence challenges nearly every police officer, quickly and repeatedly. I respect the courage it took to write this book as well as the courage to deal with the devil over the course of your career. I will be looking for opportunities to make use of your book in my work with both police agencies and law students.

Michael S. Scott, University of Wisconsin Law School
Director, Center for Problem-Oriented Policing

Michael Quinn writes a courageously truthful book on police ethics in *Walking With the Devil* From a practitioner perspective, his book examines his experience during his career with the Minneapolis Police Department. As we enter the 21st Century, the book should be a "Rosetta Stone" for practitioners in Policing a Free Society whether from Baghdad to Bloomington. The book is an excellent resource for academia and instructors in the field of criminal justice.

Michael F. Gorham, Deputy Sheriff
Wisconsin DOJ Training and Standards
Curriculum Committee Member

Quinn's book reveals what really goes on behind the scenes. I learned stuff I never knew, including about one case I handled in the grand jury. Quinn describes police falsifying reports, committing perjury, and covering these acts by the "Code of Silence." It's cover your partner's ass, because next time you may need the partner to cover yours. When Quinn saw misconduct, he went to superiors, first line supervising sergeants, lieutenants, and even deputy chiefs, getting no satisfaction. So, what's so important about this book? It is that every judge should read it and understand the pressures and motivation that foster the police misconduct that defense lawyers see every day. Let's face it, these judges are incredibly naïve about police misconduct. They think the police tell the truth and defendants lie. When I was a third year law student doing a prosecutorial intern-ship I was assigned a marijuana possession case. The defendant was arrested in his living room and the police found the pot in the bedroom. This was just after the Supreme Court decided *Chimel v. California* in which the court said a "search incident" was limited to the arrestee's arm's reach. When I told this to the cop who seized the evidence, he said, "Well, then, I found the pot in the living room." Needless to say I was shocked at his readiness to commit perjury and dismissed the case. Quinn details case after case of this sort of thing. Quinn makes the point that "one cop" can make a difference. He cites examples in which misbehaving police were told by cowork-ers to stop. The misconduct would stop in front of the complainant. Color me cynical, but who knows what happened elsewhere. Read this book and pass it on to the bench. It is a rare glimpse at a world that is indeed shrouded in the "Code of Silence."

John C. Brink, Attorney
Former Hennepin County Prosecutor
2003-2010 Super Lawyer

I thought I would take today to tell you that I think you have written a great book. It is sorely need in the law enforcement community. Its greatest value is that it will generate heated debates and offend those who need to be offended. I always liked and admired you. I appreci-ated your drive and competency. Today I admire your courage!

William J. Lewinski, PhD.
Force Science® Institute, Ltd

Quinn challenges ethical officers with a simple, practical strategy for confronting an unethical environment. *Walking With the Devil* instills a sense of hope for cracking the blue code of silence. I recently referenced Quinn's concepts as I taught police ethics to the command staff of a police agency in a developing country. Without a doubt, Quinn's message is universal. A powerful read for those who believe in the ethical obligations of the police.

Chief Frank Kaminski (ret)
Evanston, Illinois Police Department

I just purchased, read (in one sitting), highlighted and footnoted your excellent book on the Police Code of Silence—I found absolutely nothing therein, with which I did not completely agree! I retired as Chief of Police for the city Bellevue, WA (a twin city of Seattle somewhat akin to St. Paul and Minneapolis). To me the great mystery of law enforcement has always been why 98% of our police officers do a difficult job well but will cover-up for the other 2%, with whom we would all be better off without—Mike Quinn has helped to explain why and how that occurs. Congratulations on an important statement that should be required reading for every Chief of Police, Prosecutor, and Judge in the United States.

D.P. "Van" Blaricom
Chief of Police—Retired, Police Practices Expert

It's absolutely outstanding, but also sobering. As a retired career cop (Michigan) and a Field Training Instructor since 1982, I can attest to the imprinting that FTO/Mentors have on Probationers. Keep writing—it's an important gap to fill! With the best wishes, Coach Sok—

Bruce A. Sokolove
Law Enforcement Consultant, Field Training Associates

I have known Mike Quinn for many years now and worked with him in several capacities. Whatever the issue, and whatever his function Quinn is always the epitome of professionalism. As a security professional his attention to to detail and to duty are always dialed in. As a tactical trainer he is a real expert but still flexible enough to listen to new ideas. As an author and speaker on ethics issues Quinn is highly principled, yet thoughtful and compassionate. I highly recommend his book for anyone that cares to honestly explore the complexities of ethics in the context of life and death issues on the street.

Glen Legus, U.S. Marshal's Service

By way of introduction, My name is Larry Horak. I'm a long time city cop and former FBI agent. I just wanted to convey to you my appreciation for your excellent take on the police code of silence. I saw many parallels between your experiences and those that I encountered throughout my career. During my career, I've been put in unenviable positions due to indiscretions taken by those with whom I worked Fortunately, I chose to the right thing and lived to see another workday.

I currently teach police internal affairs for the FBI Law Enforcement Executive Development Association (LEEDA) and I mention and recommend your book during the module of the course that deals with the code of silence.

At any rate, kudos to you and thanks for putting on paper what's been bouncing around my own head for many years.

Larry Horak, Margate (FL) Police Department
Professional Standards Division

It's a good, fun read that gets to the heart of dealing with issues of mistrust of the police in our communities of color. I would recommend it to any one who is interested in such issues, or who is attempting to deal with them. If I were teaching our Police and Community course, it would be required reading in that!

Dr. Scott Magnuson-Martinson, Chair
Sociology, Anthropology and Law Enforcement
Normandale Community College, Bloomington, MN

Thank you for sending me your book to review. Just by way of background, I have been with the California Commission of Peace Officer Standards and Training for over 7 years. During that time I have worked with every rank from Sergeant to Chief on leadership and ethics.

I found your book absolutely fascinating. It was the best book on the topic I have read. The stories were riveting, the analysis and research excellent, and the relevance to policing right on target. I have passed the book on to a couple of colleagues, one of which I expect will contact you shortly.

Steve Lewis, Senior Law Enforcement Consultant
Commission on Peace Officer Standards and Training, California

Dear Mr. Quinn:
Your book has been placed in the Office of the Chancellor library. Please know that this fine work reflects upon and redounds to the benefit of the entire Minnesota State Colleges and Universities system. With best wishes,

James H. McCormick, Chancellor
Minnesota State Colleges and Universities

Thanks for writing it Mike. People need to know that this kind of stuff still goes on. It took guts for you to write it. People give the same excuse they always do. "Oh, that was back in the bad old days." They said that in the seventies, too. Also, people need to know that it's not just New York and Chicago.

Mark G. Robbins, PhD
Dept. of Political Science/Law Enforcement
MN State Colleges and Universities

A truly courageous book that brings to light the seductive power of the Code and the false belief that one cannot step back after crossing the line. A powerful book. It caused me to recognize and rethink my personal transgressions with code and vow that I never again allow its seductive power to take hold in my life. A must-read for every officer. An empowering work that helps the officer to look at himself in the mirror at the end of each shift without shame, remorse, or regret.

James F. Zagrzebski
U.S. Marine Corps Military Police (Retired)
MTC Police (Retired)

The "10 Myths" were excellent and should be taught, learned and become part of the police culture.

Michael A. CampionPhD, LP, HSPP, CPQ.
Campion, Barrow and Associates, Champaign, Illinois

I found your book to be fascinating, informative and powerful. Once I started reading it I couldn't put it down. It gave me an adrenaline rush.

Patricia J. Hughes, Attorney at Law
Former Executive Director
Minneapolis Police Civilian Review Authority

Everyone in the Criminal Justice System needs to read this book!

Steven Gilkerson, FBI, Retired
Former SWAT Commander

Michael W. Quinn's new book, *Walking With the Devil: The Police Code of Silence,* is a must-read for every ethical person involved with the legal system. Quinn writes in vivid street-cop language, compelling police recuits'—and our—attention with gritty adrenaline-laced descriptions of the life-and-death, "slippery with blood and sweat" survival-mode situations in which gut instincts—"amygdala hijackings"—propel even the most ethical cops into difficult battles with the Code of Silence, the implicit rule that a cop never 'snitches' on another cop. When he has our attention, he leads us through the "terrible internal struggles" of honesty and ethics. Quinn is bluntly honest about "cop culture" and institutional pressures toward corruption, including "creative report writing" and "testilying." Quinn guides his readers into a gut-level understanding of real-life ethics. He addresses the criminally-serious problems detailed in his book, describing outstanding successes of two police units he supervised, "that refused to use the Code," and debunks the 'top ten' "Myths of Policing." The Police Code of Silence is a profoundly powerful text book. When studied with the dedicated seriousness of a police recruit at the Academy, Michael Quinn's teaching builds and strengthens ethics beyond abstract intellectual knowledge, into the very fibers of one's being. Even in those of us who believe ourselves to deeply ethical, Quinn's book can awaken and nurture a deeper understanding of ethics as a vital part of life in every moment.

Clara NiiSka
Guest Reviewer
National Lawyers Guild Chapter News

The Police
Code of Silence

WALKING WITH THE DEVIL

WHAT BAD COPS DON'T WANT YOU TO KNOW
AND GOOD COPS WON'T TELL YOU

Michael W. Quinn

Minneapolis Police, Retired

Quinn and Associates

Minneapolis

Edited by Margot T. Willett, Ed.D.
Cover design by Matt Butzow and Michael Quinn
Book design by Dorie McClelland, www.springbookdesign.com
Author photo by Diane Griffin, Precision Imaging Studio

Books are available from:
Partners Book Distributing Inc., 2325 Jarco Drive, Holt, Michigan 48842, (517)-694-3205, amazon.com, barnesandnoble.com, and booksbyquinn.com. Desk Copies and Teacher's Guide CD may be obtained directly from Michael Quinn at mike@booksbyquinn.com.
Library of Congress Control Number: 2004095119
SAN: 256-1824
ISBN 978-0-9759125-2-2 hardcover
ISBN 978-0-9759125-3-9 trade softcover
ISBN 978-0-9759125-2-6 hardcover library binding
Second edition

Michael Quinn is available for your conference or community training to speak on *Walking with the Devil, the Police Code of Silence* and Survival Ethics. You can contact Mike at Mikeqisjpn@msn.com.

DEDICATION

For Sara, my wife and best friend, my children, Mom and Dad, my brothers and sisters, the officers of the Minneapolis Police Department, and all my non-police friends who helped me stay sane and make sense out of senseless acts.

CONTENTS

No rats   *xi*

Introduction   *xiii*

A Police Family Heritage   *1*

The Code of Silence   *3*
Silent cops   *3*
A twisted relationship   *6*

The Reality of the Code   *13*
Officer needs help   *13*
We do cover for each other   *19*
The only thing that matters   *21*
The gut reaction—the amygdala hijak   *28*

Policing as an Ideal   *35*
From blue uniform to blue uniform   *35*
When cops are thieves   *37*
There are worse things than thieves   *41*
The adrenaline fix   *44*
Even the best training is not enough   *47*

A Day in the Life   *51*
What did you do today daddy?   *51*
It all starts here   *57*

Committed to the truth   67

Police academy—this is a test   70

Internal affairs   75

The Narcotics Investigator   79

Undercover work   79

Cops already know who's guilty   83

Mixing the truth with small lies   85

The entry   86

What could possibly go wrong?   88

Creative report writing—masters level   102

Our recent history—it's not pretty   110

The ripple effect   113

Collaborative power   117

Teaching ethics to cops—or not   119

The Code at the executive level   120

Trusting in your partners   121

The best job in my career   125

Ten Myths of Policing   127

The street way   127

Myth 1: Street justice teaches people a lesson   129

Myth 2: The courts won't punish people
so the police must   133

Myth 3: Cops who deal with a lot of bad guys
always draw a lot more complaints   135

Myth 4: Swearing and cursing are necessary
in police work   139

Myth 5: Use of racial or other derogatory slurs
    is OK as long as it is not on the job   *140*

Myth 6: Once you are in the Code of Silence
    group, you can't get out   *141*

Myth 7: Tougher law enforcement is the answer   *144*

Myth 8: Leadership means you have to be promoted
    and be the toughest SOB on the shift   *146*

Myth 9: People only respect what they fear   *148*

Myth 10: You need to be macho to be a good cop   *150*

Now What Do We Do?   *155*

The police chief and plausible deniability   *155*

The future of criminal justice ethics training   *159*

No cop is all good or all bad   *182*

Friendly fire   *183*

And Then There Is the Law   *185*

Newspaper Columns   *193*

Notes   *257*

Glossary   *259*

References   *265*

Index   *275*

ACKNOWLEDGMENTS

After reading my book a student wanted to know where I got the strength to stand up to the Code. The answer is easy: my mother. She was the most forgiving and loving person I've ever known. She taught me that skin of a different color and different sexual preferences are just that—different. They aren't good or bad in and of themselves. She taught me to look beyond the differences and see the person.

Life is messy and we must experience it for ourselves and practice applying those lessons if we are to succeed. Just as importantly, we must realize that we can't do it alone. We must depend on, lean on, learn from, listen to, and accept the advice and help of others. I want to acknowledge some of the people who supported me and made a difference in my life. Dad was in law enforcement for 40 years. He told me many times over that your integrity was the one thing only *you* could lose. No one could take it from you. Thanks Dad, you were right.

I want to thank some of my law enforcement partners and friends: Dick Gardner, who taught me more about police work than anyone before or since. Thank you Don Schwartz, for saving my life on more than one occasion and Al Garber and Steve Gilkerson for teaching me the real meaning of leadership. Brian Carlson, Sally Beel, Kim Coughlin, Mick Leone, DuWayne Walker, and Ron Bellendier for your professionalism and the incredible effort you put into the Minneapolis Police Academy. To the men and women of the

Minneapolis Police Department, especially the Decoy Unit, Repeat Offender Program, Emergency Response Unit, and my good friend Greg Hestness, thank you, it was an honor working with you.

I want to thank the Minnesota State Patrol for the opportunity to work in the Police Corps Program. No one ever worked harder or smarter than Lt. Steve Willars, Sergeant Warren Ackerson, Vicki Otto, and Heather Olson to make that program a reality.

Thanks to Margot Willet for her help and her friendship. She is listed as editor but she was much more than that. She has been my mentor, advisor, and cheer leader throughout this whole process. This book would not have come about without her. To Kären Hess, thanks for your advice and support. Many thanks to all those folks who read my various versions of manuscripts over the last two years. Your input was invaluable.

Dorie McClelland of Spring Book Design, you're the best.

To my friends and family, especially my personal hero and youngest brother, SFC Hugh Quinn, Iraq War Vet, I say thank you for keeping me sane and helping me try to make sense out of senseless acts; for reminding me that the world is mostly good, not bad; and for being there when I needed your advice and friendship. I could not have done it without you.

I want to thank my son Michael and his wife Kessea, and their beautiful girls Alex and Jessie, my daughter Molly and her husband Troy, and their wonderful children Devon, Alora, and Garrett. To all of you: You are more than I deserve.

Finally, I want to thank my wife Sara for just being herself. She has been my rudder and from time to time my captain and always, always, my best friend.

NO RATS

As Peace Officers we willingly lay our lives on the line for each other and the public we serve. Yet, we walk away or turn our heads when we see another officer doing something that could end their career, their marriage, or their freedom. Because we don't "rat" on another peace officer.

AS OFFICERS we have taken an oath to protect and serve the public and each other. Yet, the number of officers that commit suicide is much greater than the number of officers killed by felons. Some of those suicides are the result of being under investigation for crimes or unethical behavior. Behavior that other cops were aware of and never reported, and did nothing to stop, because we don't "rat" on other cops.

AS DEPUTIES, we have sworn to protect those in our custody. Yet some of us will go to prison every year because of acts that could have, and should have, been stopped by other deputies because we don't "rat" on other deputies.

AS TROOPERS, we have sworn to protect and serve by keeping our highways safe. Yet some of us will die in traffic accidents because we drive too fast for all the wrong reasons and some of us will be stopped, but not arrested, for drunk driving because we don't "rat" on other troopers.

AS SPECIAL AGENTS, we have sworn to uphold the constitution. Yet some of us will go to prison this year because we did nothing when we saw other agents involved in criminal or unethical behavior because we don't "rat" on other agents.

AS GUARDS, we protect each other against men and women convicted of the most heinous crimes. But we will ignore unethical or even criminal conduct of other guards. Because we don't "rat" on other guards.

There is a code of silence in the criminal justice system that infects all levels, and the cost in lives destroyed or lost is enormous. It is not an infection we can cure, but it is an infection we can fight, by making a commitment to protect each other against ourselves as well as others.

Michael W Quinn—Sergeant,
Minneapolis Police Department, Retired

INTRODUCTION

Technically, I am a *retired* cop but, in my heart, I will always *be* a cop. The job does that, leaving you with memories of glorious moments mixed with the physical and emotional scars of your battles lost. And you are changed. This book is about my battles— won and lost—with the Code of Silence. These are real stories, about real crimes, committed by real cops. Every day in our newspapers we can find another instance of police abuse of authority or criminal behavior. Our police chiefs will tell you these are the "bad apples" or the "pockets of corruption" representing only a very small number of our officers, and they're right. "It is only a few." But while they are a minority, they're a handicap the rest of us have learned to live with for far too long. That's the problem. Too many good cops have learned, through the Code of Silence, to tolerate bad cops and too many bad apples have escaped consequences as a result.

This isn't a local or regional problem. It is a nationwide problem that is undermining the quality and legitimacy of good police work. For example, the issues around the Rodney King police brutality case are not unique to L.A. They are symptomatic of a nationwide change in police philosophy from "protect and serve" to "convict and incarcerate." This is a direct result of the ongoing, uphill war against drugs. "Creative report writing" and "testi-lying" in court have become a commonplace practice as a means of ensuring that drug dealers are convicted and incarcerated. I know that most cops don't start their careers believing the ends justify the means—so how do they get that way?

The explanation isn't easy. There is no one description that fits all cops. We are men and women of all shapes, colors, sizes and philosophies, and the Code of Silence affects us all. We are a family of "blue" when it comes to the job, and we are a close-knit community in ways that only those who share extreme danger can understand. The elements that bind us so powerfully also make us defensive and resentful when we are questioned about our performance. Sometimes we fail to recognize how often we, the first line of defense in the criminal justice system, contribute to the problems that we so vehemently condemn.

We all make mistakes, and somewhere, sometime, we all "Walk with the Devil." We buy into the Code of Silence, but it doesn't have to rule, or ruin, our careers. I know from my own experience that you can see that *walk* for what it really is, an amoral perversion of the truth. The Code of Silence is about lies and deception. It lies to the community and deceives them about what cops are doing, and it lies to the cops who use it and deceives them about what they are accomplishing.

Contrary to what some will say, this book is not about judging cops. I wrote this book because I love cops. We are family and, like family, I am duty and honor bound to those who helped me find my way. Now I am in a position to help others find their way. If I did not, if I quit now, I would be as guilty as those who use the Code of Silence to cover their illegal acts.

For twenty-three and a half years I was a member of the Minneapolis Police Department and for a year and a half I was part of the Police Corps Program. My impetus for writing this book comes from seeing some of the good men and women I trained losing their careers and wasting their lives because of bad decisions: decisions that might have been different if their partners, or trainers, had done the right thing and stopped them before it was too late.

It also comes in part from second guessing myself. As I saw officers arrested for crimes or suspended for violations of department rules I had to ask, "Where does our training fail these eager recruits and their trainers that they have gone so far astray?" The answer I kept coming back to was the Code of Silence.

The Code of Silence is seductive and powerful, but it is also vulnerable. When you understand the physical, social, and psychological origins of the Code you will see through the seduction, and you will know it for what it really is—an amoral perversion of the truth.

Successful lives and successful communities are built on truth, not lies and deception. We can do the job the way it is supposed to be done. We owe it to the community. We owe it to ourselves.

A Police Family Heritage

OURS IS A FAMILY OF COPS. My dad was a cop. I was a cop. My sister is a cop. My brother-in-law and his wife were cops. For over forty years Dad was involved in the law enforcement community with twenty years on the Minneapolis force. He did it because he saw a need. He felt he could do something important to help. He knew there were people who, through no fault of their own, were living desperate lives and he wanted to be there to help them.

He clearly wasn't in it for the money. With ten kids, his police salary was stretched very thin. But no matter how tough things were in our house, he only had to go to work to see people struggling in circumstances much worse than ours.

Dad had deep feelings about what he did, and when he retired he took on the job of leading the Law Enforcement Training Program at Hibbing Community College. To this day his old students, many now chiefs and sheriffs, talk about how important it was to them to have Dad as a mentor and teacher.

After winning national recognition for his achievements at the school, he worked for the County Sheriff's Office Boat and Water

Patrol. In the worst kind of weather he would go out on the lake and look for lost boaters and, all too often, he worked with divers to recover the body of a fisherman or duck hunter who didn't see the necessity of a life vest. But even that wasn't enough for him.

When the Safe and Sober program was looking for someone to help organize law enforcement agencies to target drunk drivers, Dad jumped at the opportunity, having lost a daughter to a drunk driver in front of his house.

Dad was retired and volunteering at the local hospital because they need help. During a lunch break in the hospital cafeteria, Dad noticed a woman who was turning blue. No one at her table understood what was happening, but Dad did. He approached her and asked the questions all emergency service personnel learn to ask: Are you in trouble? Can you talk? Can you breathe? When the answers came with only shakes and nods of her head, Dad stood her up, performed the Heimlich maneuver and out popped a large piece of meat. She took a few minutes to compose herself and then left the cafeteria. Dad's only comment was, "I was lucky to be in the right place at the right time."

Service to others, that was my dad. That's what I grew up believing, and still believe, is the essence of police work.

The Code of Silence

It is necessary only
for the good man
to do nothing
for evil to triumph.

EDMUND BURKE (1729–1797), IRISH-BORN WHIG POLITICIAN

SILENT COPS

WE DON'T LIKE TO TALK ABOUT the Code of Silence. Too often it brings up memories of events we've tried to forget or cop crimes we witnessed—or committed. Asking us to talk about what we have seen or done under cover of the Code is like asking a complete stranger to share their most intimate fantasy. It's not going to happen. But the Code is well known by all—from the chief on down. It allows some cops to operate unethically, even criminally, and it prevents good cops from stopping them.

The National Institute of Justice reported that in a "nationally representative telephone survey of 925 randomly selected American police officers from 121 departments," 52.4 percent of the officers agreed, "It is not unusual for a police officer to turn a blind eye to improper conduct by other officers." In that same study, 61 percent disagreed with the statement "Police officers always report serious criminal violations involving abuse of authority by fellow officers."

A surprising 6 in 10 (60 percent) indicated that police officers do not always report even serious criminal violations that involve the abuse of authority by fellow officers. (Weisbrud 2000, 3–4)

Put another way: only 39 percent of police officers believe fellow officers will report serious criminal violations involving the abuse of authority.

That is the Code of Silence—the singularly most powerful influence on police behavior in the world.

But 61 percent or even 100 percent, these percentages mean little to the street cop where the first priority every night is to stay alive, and the minimum dress code is body armor and high-capacity firearms. Small towns or big cities, it's easy to forget you swore an oath to be a *peace* officer when someone is trying to kill you just because you wear a badge. Take these examples from the National Law Enforcement Officers Memorial Fund.

Brian Gibson, a 27-year-old police officer in Washington, D.C. was gunned down as he sat at a traffic light in his marked police cruiser. It was a cold-blooded assassination. It was also a shocking reminder of just how vulnerable our police officers can be.

Unfortunately, Officer Gibson's death is not as rare as we'd like to think. Throughout history, more than 1,200 police officers have been ambushed and killed in unprovoked attacks. In the 1990s we were averaging 21 police assassinations per year.

One of those fallen heroes was Jerry Haaf, a Minneapolis police officer who was shot in the back while having a cup of coffee. It happened during the early morning hours of September 25, 1992.

Officer Haaf was nearing the end of his shift and he stopped by a favorite cop hangout to get a cup of coffee and finish some paper-work. He never saw the two gang members enter the dimly-lit restaurant. He didn't even have a chance to draw his weapon. The murderers quickly walked up behind him, shot him twice in the back, and then ran out the door. The entire incident lasted less than 30 seconds.

The FBI reports that in 2008

> while serving in the line of duty, 41 law enforcement
> officers were feloniously killed. Another 77 officers died
> as the result of duty-related accidents, and at least 58,792
> others were victims of some type of assault. (FBI Uniform
> Crime Reports)

Every day is a new challenge and ethical police conduct is often an uphill battle. Even the best of cops have days when they want to give up and do whatever it takes to put a child molester, baby mur-derer, or other lowlife in prison. When you sit inches away from these scum and they brag about the truly horrific things they have done to an innocent, it's easy to abide by the Code—if that's what it takes. When the evidence isn't perfect, you just use a little creative report writing and this guy will never harm another person again. Illegal searches, physical abuse, or even perjury, you know you will be in the company of many good cops who have done the same. But are they *really* good cops?

And is it worth losing your honor, integrity, and possibly your job? What about your family? Are you willing to sacrifice them, too? Because when the world finds out in the local news what you did, will you be able to explain to them why you were willing to be a criminal just to lock up another criminal? Can you do that?

A TWISTED RELATIONSHIP

Most cops will spend more time talking to their partners than they will with their spouses, kids, or significant others. In many ways we are in a marriage of convenience with our coworkers. Publicly confronting them about criminal or unethical behavior is like testifying against your spouse; you know if you make their secrets public, they will make yours public. Besides, there are rules against it— The Code of Silence—which may be unwritten, but will be enforced. And if you break those rules, the sentence for going public includes everything from being shunned to losing your job.

The cop on the street witnesses daily the murder and mayhem going on around this country. Constitutional boundary lines that were so clear in the classroom become blurred in the face of violent, senseless acts that we are helpless to stop.

The Bureau of Justice reports that in 2009

> • An estimated 4.3 million violent crimes, 15.6 million
> property crimes, and 133,000 personal thefts were com-
> mitted against U.S. residents age 12 or older in 2009.
> • Violence against males, blacks, and persons age 24 or
> younger occurred at higher or somewhat higher rates
> than the rates of violence against females, whites, and
> persons age 25 or older in 2009.
> • About half (49%) of all violent crimes and about 40% of
> all property crimes were reported to the police in 2009.
> Violent crimes against females (53%) were more likely to
> be reported than violent crimes against males (45%).[1]

And the Code, the *Almighty Code,* which pays no heed to constitutional limits, gives us the power to incarcerate and punish at
will the subhuman trash responsible for these statistics; and it feels
good. In our out-of-control world on the street, it gives us a sense of
control. Omissions, lies, and deception in reports and testimony—
when carefully mixed with the truth—become the weapons of
choice in the war on crime. And they are devastating, on the crime
rate and the community.

But, if our communities knew the truth, they would not
approve of some of the things we do in the name of justice. Because
while we are busy congratulating ourselves on the effectiveness of
our tactics, it is the community that pays the price for our deception in a loss of community trust and a dismantling of families in
our minority communities. Across the country our "war on drugs"
is having devastating effects.

Look at what happened in Hennepin County, or more precisely, Minneapolis, Minnesota, as reported in the African American Men Project Final Report (2002).

> When young African American men do poorly, they are not the only ones who suffer; every person, family and business in the county also pays a price in the form of a continued labor shortfall, limited economic development, reduced tax revenues, higher crime, and higher costs for social services, law enforcement and county courts. These costs, totaling hundreds of millions of dollars each year, reduce the overall quality of life for everyone in the county. . . .
>
> This report focuses on Hennepin County's young African American men, especially those who live in the five poorest communities in Minneapolis. Many of these men are in trouble—with money, with employment, with their families, with their health, and with the criminal justice system.
>
> This trouble stems from a web of interrelated and mutually reinforcing causes. As a result, many of these men are unable to create much social, political, economic, or human capital for themselves.
>
> A wide range of individuals and organizations in Hennepin County have a direct stake in the success of these men. This echoes a simple but often-overlooked reality: what is good for young African American men is good for the county, and vice versa. (One obvious example: when the local economy thrives, the unemploy-

ment rate among this group drops dramatically; when the economy does poorly, these men are typically among the first to lose their jobs.)

What is good for young African American men is also good for families: fathers who are employed and financially stable are much more likely to get married, stay married, and fulfill their roles as fathers. The central question posed by this report is, "How can young African American men and Hennepin County help each other succeed?" For years, there have been many mechanisms in place to benefit 18- to 30-year-old African American men. Yet the outcomes for many of these men continue to be poor. For example:

- Forty-four percent are arrested each year.
- They are 27 times more likely to go to jail than young white men.
- [Only] twenty-eight percent of these young men enrolled in the Minneapolis Public Schools graduate from high school in four years.
- They are twice as likely as young white men 18 to 30 years old to die.

If you are an African American male, age 18–30, living in Hennepin County:

No matter where you live in Hennepin County, you're probably doing about as well as your counterparts in many other large American cities and counties. This is the conclusion of a study commissioned for this report and conducted by the University of Minnesota's Institute on Race and Poverty. For this study, researchers collected demographic, socioeconomic and educational summary data from the mid- and late 1990s for 11 metro areas (and, in some cases, the states in which these cities are located):

- Atlanta
- Baltimore
- Cleveland
- Denver
- Miami
- Minneapolis
- Phoenix
- Portland (OR)
- St. Louis
- San Diego
- Seattle

The study looked at how you and other African Americans are faring according to a variety of measures: school dropout rates by race and gender; performance of eighth graders in writing and basic math by race; unemployment by race; incarceration rates by race and gender; and death rates by race and ethnicity.

This study concluded:

- In every area studied, outcomes and conditions for African Americans were significantly poorer than those for whites.
- The conditions and outcomes for Hennepin County African Americans were about average for the 11 metro areas examined.

We all know that we can't hold cops accountable for all our social ills. However, we can and must look at how a policy of "convict and incarcerate" contributes to the mix, and we cannot deny our responsibility for the consequences.

Tulia, Texas—15 percent of the town's African American population arrested on drug charges. "These cases were all based on the uncorroborated testimony of hired investigator Tom Coleman. It was determined that a number of the people Coleman arrested were not even in Tulia at the time Coleman claims the crimes were committed. The cases were eventually vacated and Coleman was convicted of perjury."

Seattle, Washington—Using statistical evidence compiled by graduate students at Harvard's Kennedy School of Government, the attorneys argue that the narcotics offenses are racist in intent and consequences.

Los Angeles, California—Known as the Rampart Scandal, over a hundred convictions were overturned as police misconduct, ranging from the planting of evidence to "confessions" obtained through beatings was uncovered.

Toronto, Canada—Toronto police Chief Julian Fantino has called in the Mounties to head a probe into allegations of perjury and theft in an ever-widening police corruption scandal that has plagued the force for years.

Cops are not blind to this corruption. We see what is happening. But too few of us are looking for ways to stop it. Many believe increased educational requirements and better on-the-job training will produce more ethical cops. Maybe—maybe not.

The problem with classroom ethics lectures is that they seldom depict the reality of the street. Ethical decision-making in a classroom setting, except on rare occasions, is a farce and we know it. As much as we complain about it, cops like the classroom ethics training because there are no negative consequences. We can say all the right things and we don't have to change our behavior; so we don't.

In fact, many cops choose to believe they have a mandate from their community, and their chiefs, to do whatever it takes to lock up criminals. Ethics be damned; it's about justice and the safety of the community. In some cases we have that mandate from the community.

But communities that allow their cops to ignore the rules and marginalize any part of the community are only trading one form of violence for another—and it is a bad trade. You cannot separate individual justice from community justice. It is a symbiotic relationship. Like an injury to the human body, an injury to the justice system at the personal level is an injury to the body of the community.

To "protect and serve," that is our real mandate. If there is going to be pain and injury, it should be the result of our efforts to carry out that mandate, not the result of violating it. No matter how hard we try, innocents will suffer and evil will occasionally win. We cannot protect everyone, everywhere, and there will always be some pain in the community. The community understands that.

What they cannot understand, and should not tolerate, are protectors that are the cause of their pain.

The Reality of the Code

Between the idea

And the reality

Between the motion

And the act

Falls the Shadow

T.S. ELIOT, "THE HOLLOW MEN," 1925

OFFICER NEEDS HELP

UNFORTUNATELY OR REALISTICALLY, as often as not it is another cop's actions that causes us to embrace the Code. No matter how cautious or smart we think we are, every cop gets in over his head at some time and has to call for help. When the "officer needs help" call goes out, other cops will make incredible efforts and take crazy risks to get to you in time. Seconds can mean the difference between life and death. But the Code of Silence can produce ethical dilemmas for the officers involved in an "officer needs help" call. Responding cops often physically shake with an adrenaline rush that only fuels our anger toward anyone or anything that dares to threaten the safety of a cop.

As we arrive on the scene of a "help" call, we are capable of anything and everything to help a fellow officer—including the use of extreme force.

> The use of force is a relatively rare occurrence in American policing, but previous studies suggest that when it does occur, it may often escalate to the level of excessive force. (Weisbrud, 2)

Here is an example of what can happen. Pretend for a moment that you are the cop in the following scenario. This is a composite event not meant to represent any one event or any individual cop.

Working alone, you get a call to a violent domestic—one of the most dangerous calls we face. It's in the middle of the street just around the corner from your location. You know you should wait for backup, but the dispatcher says she can hear a woman screaming "Don't kill me!" so you go. There really is no other choice.

> • In 2008 the rate of intimate partner victimizations for females was 4.3 victimizations per 1,000 females age 12 or older. The equivalent rate of intimate partner violence against males was 0.8 victimizations per 1,000 males age 12 or older.

- The rate of intimate partner violence against females declined 53% between 1993 and 2008, from 9.4 victimizations per 1,000 females age 12 or older to 4.3 per 1,000.
- Against males, the rate declined 54%, from 1.8 victimizations per 1,000 males age 12 or older to 0.8 per 1,000. Between 1993 and 2007 the overall rate of female homicides fell 43% from 4.18 to 2.38 homicides per 100,000 female U.S. residents.[2] (Intimate Violence, Bureau of Justice Statistics)

As you drive up and slide to a stop, you see a big man kneeling on the ground, hitting a small woman with his right fist in her bloody face. His left hand is wrapped up in her long hair pinning her head to the street. Your adrenaline kicks in and you immediately go ballistic. Bailing from the squad, you call for backup and run up to the man.

As you get closer you see they are both covered in blood. It's clear there are some serious injuries. He stops punching the woman but does not let her go. You grab him by his right arm and suddenly realize how big he really is, but it's too late. His arm, wet and slippery with blood and sweat, easily breaks your grip. He stands up as you move in to grab him, and you step into a sucker punch from his left fist. You can feel yourself falling to the ground but you can't stop it. At first there is no pain, just a sudden confusion about where you are and what you are doing. It's like trying to wake up from a bad dream combined with a brutal hangover. You find yourself on your hands and knees. You can taste the salty-sweet blood in your mouth. You know you have to get up, but you aren't sure why.

You can be killed.

You see him standing over you but you can barely move. You raise your arm just in time to partially block a kick from his size 13 boot aimed directly at your head. Amazingly, you have no feelings about your actions. You are on autopilot. Your body is in survival mode and your rational mind is along just for the ride—a detached observer. You are on your back. You can hear someone calling for help. The voice is strained and scared. You don't realize it is yours.

As you struggle to stand, the next kick comes into your ribs, taking the wind completely out of you. You can hear sirens but it means nothing. You are focused on trying to breathe. Your gun is out and you have it pointed at the bad guy. You know you should shoot; he is beating you to death. He comes at you again but you can't focus; you can't breathe. As you try to point your gun, he suddenly disappears under a mob of uniforms. You are helpless; you can't catch your breath enough to get off the ground. You are able to witness what happens next.

The cops that responded to your strangled call for help are on the scene, realizing you are in big trouble.

> The hormones we secrete under stress are enough for a
> single bout of fight or flight, but once secreted, they stay
> in the body for hours, and each successive upsetting
> incident adds more stress hormones to the levels already
> there. The resulting buildup can make the amygdala a

hair trigger, ready to hijack us into anger or panic at the
least provocation. (Goleman 1998, 76)

They arrived just in time to see this guy kick you in your blood-
covered face as you lay next to the now unconscious bloody woman
on the street. In their rage, they jump on your attacker from behind
and beat him into the ground.

They punch, twist, choke, kick, and strike with batons and metal
flashlights until he is completely unconscious. There is no attempt
to control him. Nobody brings out handcuffs. They just hurt him.
They inflict as much pain as they can short of killing him.

Pain in every breath you take, you aren't able to talk or get to
your feet and it's all over in ten seconds.

Now someone handcuffs your bloody pulp of a *prisoner.* An
ambulance arrives and they load you up along with your prisoner
and take you both to the ER. You watch as they scramble to get an
airway and iv into your prisoner. He stops breathing enroute. He
is on a portable respirator by the time you get to the ER and he is
admitted with brain injuries and broken bones. To save him, the neu-
rosurgeons have to suck out a substantial portion of his *personality.*

When he wakes up, several weeks later, with his jaw wired shut,
he doesn't remember a thing. The female victim also has her jaw
wired. She tells investigators that he is an ex-con she befriended
while he was in prison. This was their first meeting since he made
parole. She refused to have sex with him so he started beating her,
threatening to kill her. When he pulled the phone out of the wall, she
ran into the street screaming for help. She remembers seeing your

squad arrive. She saw the bad guy knock you down and kick you. That's all she remembers before she passed out from her injuries. She never saw the backup officers arrive.

What you witnessed from the other cops was excessive force. It was both a civil and criminal violation. But, if they hadn't arrived when they did, you and the woman would probably be dead. The responding cops saved your life and hers. Are you going to run to Internal Affairs and complain because the responding cops beat up a convicted felon who was trying to kill you? Are you going to send to prison the men and women who had to save your life after you got in over your head? No, you're not.

Your fractured ribs, broken teeth, and eyes swollen shut are evidence of the beating you took. All you have to say is, "I didn't see what happened." No one will question you. For now, for this case, you will "walk with the devil" and abide by the Code. That is not to say you believe the excessive force was justified. It is never justified. And your rational brain understands that. But, it *feels* like justice in your gut. In every fiber of your being you know that he got exactly what he deserved. And you know that for this case, for every woman he ever beat, for every rape he ever committed, you will abide by the Code. This will be one of those memories you will live with; one of the mental scars you will carry and, if you're a smart cop, you will learn from this experience.

In a best case scenario, the next time you are responding to a "help call" you will get control of yourself early. You know you don't want to put another officer through the same dilemma you experienced. You owe at least that much to your fellow officers.

And taking the devil's hand to get through one battle doesn't mean you have joined sides.

WE DO COVER FOR EACH OTHER

The bottom line is, sometimes we cover for each other. For most of us there is the realization that what happened was wrong. We see our behavior as a setback, not a victory. We analyze what went wrong and try to fix it before it happens again. But, no matter how we feel or what we believe, we are judged by our actions, not our intentions, and the costs can be horrendous. When confronted with video camera footage or audio recordings, the Code becomes a trap, and the first cop to tell the truth is usually the only one to escape permanent damage.

This isn't always true, but it is true often enough that everyone caught up in the discovered lies is thinking about it. Good cops who go along with the Code, even when they see no way out and are determined to not let it happen again, are usually the last to come forward with the truth.

But cops accustomed to using the Code are quick to recognize an out for themselves by being the first to approach the investigators about their role in the incident. They will step forward as if they want to come clean and then lie to protect themselves. Some are experts at mixing the truth with lies and sometimes they get away with it. I saw it over and over again while working in Internal Affairs and testifying at Civilian Review hearings.

Rafael Perez, the former Los Angeles police officer who
blew the whistle on a secret cabal of policemen who
routinely beat, shot, and framed innocent people, was
sentenced Friday to five years in prison for stealing
cocaine from an evidence room. Perez got his sentence cut
in half for turning against fellow officers. (LAPD Whistleblower Gets Prison Term. UPI, February 26, 2000)

I once testified in a Civilian Review hearing in direct opposition
to the testimony of the chief's aide. He was defending the actions of
the accused officers. He was, like myself, a sergeant who had worked
at the academy prior to my assignment there. He told the panel the
inappropriate behavior of the accused officers was what they had
been taught at the academy while he was there. He minimized any
personal responsibility or common sense on the part of the officers
involved. The panel believed him, not me. I wasn't surprised. I've
heard cops from across the nation voice the opinion: "I'd rather go
in front of civilian review than Internal Affairs." I could see why. The
panel members were completely taken in by the chief's aide.

Good cops will always struggle with the Code and even the
best of us will fall into its clutches. But the Code is beatable. It only
takes one cop to say, "No, not in front of me," to end the game
before it starts. And even though bad cops will swear allegiance to
each other over the "Holy Jack of Daniels," there is a breaking point
for each of them because they can never really trust each other.
Given the choice between prison and telling the truth about their
partners in crime, they will talk.

THE ONLY THING THAT MATTERS

You will hear cops say, "The only thing that really matters is that you and your partner go home at the end of the shift." And that's a true statement, but it's not all there is. Because even though we know there are people who, given the opportunity, would kill us without a second thought, we work very hard to prevent that from happening. In officer survival training, we learn a variety of mental and physical survival strategies, including how to call on our "will to live."

But, for the inexperienced cop, this "will to live" training can result in overreacting and mistakes. Let me show you how that happens. Most recruits have never been in a physical fight with another person. In our nice society, "beating up your buddy" is not a required class in any school. But cops must learn to fight or die.

The National Law Enforcement Officers Memorial Fund reports that:

- There are more than **900,000** sworn law enforcement officers now serving in the United States, which is the highest figure ever. About **12 percent** of those are female.
- In 2008, there were an estimated **4.9 million** violent crimes committed in the United States, as well as an estimated 16.3 million property crimes (according to the National Crime Victimization Survey conducted by the Bureau of Justice Statistics). Violent and property crime rates in 2008 remain at the lowest levels recorded since 1973, the first year that such data were collected. The

rate of every major violent and property crime measured by BJS fell between 1999 and 2008. The overall violent crime rate fell 41 percent and the property crime rate declined by 32 percent during the last 10 years.

- Crime fighting has taken its toll. Since the first recorded police death in 1792, there have been nearly **19,000** law enforcement officers killed in the line of duty. Currently, there are **18,983** names engraved on the walls of the National Law Enforcement Officers Memorial.

- A total of **1,626** law enforcement officers died in the line of duty during the past 10 years, an average of one death every **53** hours or **163** per year. There were **116** law enforcement officers killed in 2009, the lowest annual total since 1989.

- On average, more than **58,000** law enforcement officers are assaulted each year, resulting in approximately **16,000** injuries.

- The **1970s** were the deadliest decade in law enforcement history, when a total of **2,286** officers died, or an average of almost **229** each year. The deadliest year in law enforcement history was **1930**, when **285** officers were killed. That figure dropped dramatically in the **1990s**, to an average of **160** per year.

- The deadliest day in law enforcement history was September 11, 2001, when **72** officers were killed while responding to the terrorist attacks on America.

- New York City has lost more officers in the line of duty than any other department, with **693** deaths. Texas has lost **1,563** officers, more than any other state. The state with the fewest deaths is Vermont, with **21**.

- There are **1,002** federal officers listed on the Memorial, as well as **565** correctional officers and **29** military law enforcement officers.
- There are **237** female officers listed on the Memorial; just **one** female officer was killed in 2009, one of the lowest numbers in recent years.
- During the past ten years, more officers were killed feloniously on **Friday** than any other day of the week. The fewest number of felonious fatalities occurred on **Sunday**. Over the past decade, more officers were killed between 8:01 p.m. and and 10:00 p.m. than during any other two-hour period."[3]

In a physical confrontation with an angry *customer,* cops don't have the option of saying, "I'm not going to arrest this guy. He's too big or he looks too mean." So, to prepare new cops, we provide training that knocks them down, makes them hurt, and forces them to get back up. We make them reach down deep into their psyche and pull up all their anger and adrenaline and use it to overcome seemingly impossible odds. We do this because it can save their lives.

Here is just one example. Pete Soulis is a cop in Florida. He has been involved in several shootings but one in particular is relevant here. Pete was sitting in his squad taking a break, lights out, across the street from a convenience store. He saw a car pull up and start watching the store. The driver didn't see Pete's squad until Pete put on his lights and pulled up behind the car. The driver started to open his car door, but didn't get out. Pete decided it would be safer to approach from the passenger side, where the windows were rolled up.

When he was close enough, he aimed his flashlight into the car. The driver come up with a pistol and shot Pete in the center of the chest. Pete was wearing body armor and although the impact shocked him badly, it did not kill him. The guy in the car fired several more rounds as Pete ran for the cover of his squad returning fire at the same time. Pete was hit several times. As he crouched behind his squad car, he saw blood pumping from the bullet hole in his thigh. He believed the bullet had torn his femoral artery and he was going to die. As Pete looked at his wounds, he said to himself, "If I am going to die, this guy is going with me!" He called on all the anger and adrenaline he could muster. He stood up and moved toward the car firing continuously at the driver through the rear window. One of the final rounds hit his attacker in the back of the head and ended the gun battle, an incredible feat of officer survival.

> . . . it is well known that soldiers in battle fail to notice injuries that would, under less traumatic circumstances, be excruciatingly painful . . . pain suppression in the face of danger allows the organism to use its resources to deal with the most significant danger. (LeDoux 1996, 132)

The pictures from that night are even more telling. After being shot multiple times in this gun battle, Pete can be seen standing up and talking to the backup officers several minutes after the shooting was over. He had pumped himself up so high in his survival mode his body would not allow him to relax. This is what we try to teach our recruits. Not because we want them to be angry, but because we want them to survive, and we know this training works.

One of my former recruits was attacked on a stairway by a man with a weapon. He fell backwards and fractured his skull. He was lying on the floor and hurt so bad he just wanted to pass out to end the pain, but he didn't. He remembered a drill we did in the academy and evaluated his injuries. He saw that he was breathing and he wasn't bleeding. So he forced himself to get up and fight his attacker, subduing him just as backup arrived. He told me his training convinced him he could draw on the anger and pain to boost his adrenaline levels and fight back. It saved his life.

Any cop that has been on the street for a while will have similar, if not as dramatic, stories to tell. The problem is this. New cops in training have no frame of reference for when or where to use these techniques. We tell them the circumstances where it will be appropriate. But, until they have confronted the real possibility of death or great bodily harm in numerous situations, they don't have the experience to know how to use that survival instinct.

Of course, that lack of experience doesn't prevent them from getting those huge adrenaline surges in unfamiliar, rapidly evolving circumstances where they are unsure of the threat level, so they make a lot of mistakes as they learn to manage those surges. Only with time on the job and real experience with life-threatening situations will they develop the knowledge they need to control themselves and others in the most appropriate manner. But even experienced cops don't always do the right thing. They will sometimes *fix* their mistakes by using the Code. It is that ingrained.

When we commit that indefensible act while fighting for our own life or defending another's, it seems justifiable to revert to the Code. And, if it is all right to use it for those acts, why not use it for the smaller transgressions? After a while it becomes very easy to minimize the importance of the truth in the paperwork because the truth becomes whatever we write down and swear to. When the lie works, which it usually does, some cops see it as an affirmation of the Code.

As terrible as it is, there is no escaping the Code. It is as inevitable as your childhood diseases and just as necessary. Each stinging battle with the Code will either be an inoculation of the spirit and an opportunity to grow stronger or a crippling injury to your integrity. Regardless of the outcome, there will be vivid images you can't erase from your memory. There will always be the mental and physical scars to remind you of your battles.

But, each encounter can leave you better prepared both physically and mentally, for the tough challenges ahead, if you are willing to admit you're not superman, and you recognize your *dark side* for what it is. Because, only when we know the Code of Silence for what it is, can we gain some control over it. Either way, you won't escape unscathed because at some point in time you are going to "walk with the devil" in order to get the job done.

Michael Josephson, of the Josephson Institute of Ethics, reminds us that, although we think of ourselves in terms of our highest ideals and aspirations, we are remembered for our last worst act. This may be a good defense mechanism in terms of survival, but denying our dark side only gives the Code more power. At some point, every cop gives in to the uncontrollable rage that comes from hate and frustration, or we lie and perjure ourselves, believing it serves the greater good. And, depending on the act, other cops will cover for us.

Police ethics never have been all good or all bad, and the Code is as much a part of being a cop as the badge and the gun. But we can learn from it. Each encounter with the Code is a test of our character, but it is important to recognize that it is just a test. Being human means we will sometimes fail. But a single failure is only one step down the wrong road; it is not a commitment to follow that road. We pride ourselves on being a very close family of "blue," but somewhere along the line we have skewed those family values. We seem to have forgotten that these tests of character are and always have been family tests, and when one fails we all fail.

Of course, for some cops the Code of Silence is the road, and for them it becomes a chronic debilitating illness that cripples them and the communities where we work. The Code is based on lies and deception, it eats away at the honor and integrity of the cops who use it, it destroys the trust people have in cops, and it frustrates the community-policing efforts in our neighborhoods.

Knowing we will never eliminate it, we can prepare ourselves by analyzing how the Code of Silence works. We can know the enemy and, with that knowledge, we can be prepared to fight back.

THE GUT REACTION—AKA THE AMYGDALA HIJACK

When I started this job, I was like most new cops. I saw danger lurking around every corner and everyone I stopped was a potential serial killer. With a few years of experience, and a lack of serial killer arrests, I learned to react to threats without any conscious effort. For example, I would have my gun in hand without even thinking about taking it out of the holster. Or something I saw or heard would make the hairs stand up on the back of my neck before I figured out what I had seen. Prior experience, locked into my memory bank triggered a physical reaction before my cognitive mind was aware of what I saw.

Cops call it our *sixth* sense. It's a visceral command that comes from deep inside and directs our actions. We may not remember why, but we know we will sometimes act before having a chance to think about it. This gut reaction is a survival mechanism. In his book, *The Emotional Brain,* Joseph LeDoux explains the "fear system" that triggers this reaction.

> The system is not, strictly speaking, a system that results in the experience of fear. It is a system that detects danger and produces responses that maximize the probability of surviving a dangerous situation in the most beneficial way. It is, in other words, a system of defensive behavior. . . .
>
> We should, in other words, take defensive behaviors at face value—they represent the operation of brain systems that have been programmed by evolution to deal with danger in routine ways.

Although we can become conscious of the operation
of the defense system, especially when it leads to behav-
ioral expressions, the system operates independently of
consciousness—it is part of what we called the emotional
unconsciousness. . . ." (LeDoux 1996, 128)

This sixth sense, or fear conditioning, becomes especially fine-
tuned in cops. They don't necessarily experience a sense of fear as
much as an awareness of their physical reactions to a potential threat.
They learn to respond quickly, and sometimes aggressively.

This system (the fear system) forms implicit or nondeclar-
ative memories about dangerous or otherwise threatening
situations. Memories of this type . . . are created through
the mechanisms of fear conditioning . . . conditioned fear
responses involve implicit or unconscious processes in
two important senses: the learning that occurs does not
depend on conscious awareness and, once the learning has
taken place, the stimulus does not have to be consciously
perceived in order to elicit the conditioned emotional
responses. (LeDoux, 1996, 181–182)

A hand held behind the back or a hand reaching into the beltline under a jacket, the motorist who steps on the brakes or reaches
into the glove box as you approach—all trigger immediate reactions from experienced cops.

In worst case scenarios, there is the unexpected knife attack,
the suspect who pulls out a gun instead of his ID, or the pedestrian

who suddenly attacks you. When confronted with these potentially deadly, irrational acts, the cop who stops to reason out the cause and effect will lose his life, or someone else's. So we learn to depend on our sixth sense. We worry about the whys and wherefores later. Police field training officers who recommend termination of police recruits because of their lack of sense with regard to officer survival are often talking about the recruit's inability to tune in to their *fear system.* And they are usually right in making those recommendations. A cop needs a very sensitive fear system to survive those occasional life-threatening encounters.

One really cold winter evening, I was walking the beat downtown when a very stocky looking 5'4" male charged at me from just a few feet away, with his hand in his coat pocket, screaming, "I'm gonna kill you!"

In an instant, I threw him to my left against a parked car. Only he was a very small man in a very big coat. The force of my action launched him completely across the hood of the car into the side of a passing bus. He tumbled down the street for a few feet but, thank God, wasn't hurt. We took him to the emergency room and then to the crisis center, where he was a familiar face.

Now, admittedly, this guy was on the far end of the spectrum, but he is a great example of how quickly cops must sometimes take action. I can't say I was ever afraid of this guy. There wasn't time to be afraid or think about my actions. But I knew what I had to do, instantly.

Unfortunately, this gut reaction gives defense attorneys a lot of business because we never want to admit we acted without thinking. So we write something down to justify our actions, and if there is even the tiniest amount of physical evidence to the contrary the cop and community suffer. The cop loses credibility with the courts and is humiliated on the stand, and the community has another bad guy loose in the neighborhood.

Every cop that has been on the street for a while has done something he can't explain, not to himself or anyone else. Following a critical event, his rational mind will search for an explanation, but, if he doesn't understand why or how something happened, how can he change his behavior in the future? We can begin to make sense of this confusion by looking at the tie between our emotions and our physical reactions to highly stressful events.

In his highly acclaimed and often quoted book, *Emotional Intelligence*, Daniel Goleman calls the emotional reactions that occur without cognitive participation the "amygdala hijack."

> Such emotion explosions are neural hijackings. At those moments, evidence suggests, a center in the limbic brain proclaims an emergency, recruiting the rest of the brain to its urgent agenda.
>
> The hijacking occurs in an instant, triggering this reaction crucial moments before the neocortex, the thinking brain, has had a chance to glimpse fully what is happening, let alone decide if it is a good idea. . . . The hallmark of such a hijack is that once the moment passes, those so possessed have a sense of not knowing what came over them. (LeDoux 1996, 14)

This is a reason often quoted by cops for the necessity of the Code of Silence. In a survival mode, a rational cop may do things that are irrational, unjustified, and unexplainable. But following a "hijack," your training and the law tell you to justify your actions. There will be news media all over the event. The chief may be present, with, quite often, a police supervisor breathing down your neck to get some serious justification down on paper, even if there is none. We may even perjure ourselves, with all physical evidence to the contrary, in an effort to defend our actions. This is an especially hard time for a cop and it is critical that other cops come to their aid—not to help in fabricating lies, but supporting them in trusting in the truth.

We see it often in cases where we are involved in shootings. The law demands that we justify our actions. In deadly-force situations, we are taught that there is a reasoning process we must go through to determine if deadly force is necessary. But there isn't always time to think when someone is attempting to kill you. There may only be time to react—or you're dead. This is the basis for much of our officer survival training.

Just as important to our survival is our reliance on other cops. We expect them to put their life on the line for us just as they know we will do it for them. Ask yourself this question: how many of your friends, neighbors, or even relatives could you name who you know would absolutely risk their own life right now, this instant, to save yours? For how many of them would you risk your life? How many have actually done that for you? Mothers will do it for their children, usually, and some spouses will make that sacrifice, but the list is short in any case—unless you're a cop.

When we are fighting for our lives or fighting to save someone else's, we are still controlled by the instinct for self-survival. But to be effective, to do the things we have to do, we must consciously override that self-survival instinct, or someone dies. It's that simple. And we are ready to do it for each other every day. What kind of loyalty do you owe to someone willing to do that for you?

Policing as an Ideal

FROM BLUE UNIFORM TO BLUE UNIFORM

I JOINED THE MINNEAPOLIS Police Department at the age of 25; and for 23 years I was a Minneapolis cop. It seemed a natural progression to go from serving my country in the United States Air Force to serving my city in a police uniform. But although I'd been surrounded by law enforcement growing up, I didn't have a clue what I was getting into. I knew about helping people, but I had no clue about the extent of police corruption— drinking on the job—lying in reports—unsecured businesses that were being burglarized by cops—beating up prisoners, especially if they were Black, Indian, or drunk.

There was only one thing you *never* did. You never snitched on another cop.

The Code of Silence was the only rule you had to obey above all others. Cops didn't tell on other cops. Not for any reason. Ever!

And even the good cops, the ones you looked to for support, would turn their backs on you if you if you made a complaint about another cop. From the chief on down, you kept your mouth shut about other cops.

My introduction to the Code came early in my career. One of my first partners was a drunk. We started the 11 pm-to-7 am shift by going to a local café where the owner would pour him a couple of tall *orange juices* to go with his free piece of pie. This became a nightly ritual which occupied him for over an hour unless we got an important call. "Unimportant calls" like stolen cars, fights, or burglary alarms, he ignored until he was good and ready, which meant he had at least a .08 blood alcohol level.

Being new on the job, I did not want to be fired over this bozo's boozing, so I went to the sergeant in charge of the training officers. I told him, "I don't want to be a snitch but I don't want to lose my job." He was very supportive and the first of many supervisors to say, "I'll take care of it."

When I showed up for work the next night, nobody would talk to me. I was treated like an invisible stinking turd for the whole month. My new shoes and leather gloves disappeared from my locker. Even officers on the other shifts shunned me. An *old salt* told me it was fine not to approve of the on-the-job drinking. But he reminded me that cops never ever snitch on one another. He went on to tell me that serious *accidents* had happened to cops who snitched on other cops. That was my introduction to the Code. It was a powerful lesson.

The pervasiveness of the code of silence is bolstered by
the grave consequences for violating it: officers who
report misconduct are ostracized and harassed; become
targets of complaints and even physical threats; and are
made to fear that we will be left alone on the streets in a
time of crisis. (Mollen 1994, 53)

But then something amazing happened. Cops quit drinking
around me while they were on duty. I didn't realize the power just
one officer could have, especially a rookie. It was years later before
it occurred to me that even a rookie cop's intolerance for other
cops' bad behavior could actually have any impact on an organization. But that is exactly what happened here in a small but significant way. I saw it over and over again in my career. If just one cop
stands up and says, "No more," many cops will stop their illegal
and unethical acts in the presence of that cop. The Code of Silence
is not *the only rule*. It is vulnerable, and it takes only one cop to say,
"I'm not playing," and the game is over.

WHEN COPS ARE THIEVES

After my field training, I was assigned to a car with great partners.
I learned more in the first month with them than I did in the entire
academy. One Sunday morning my partners were off, and I worked
with an officer I did not know very well. This shift had worked
together a long time, and it had always puzzled me why my regular

partners would never want to assist any of them at DOA, burglary, or unsecured business calls. All they ever said was, "We handle our district, they handle theirs, and that is how it is done." I was about to learn the real reason.

Right out of roll call there was a burglary alarm at a fishing supply wholesaler. I started toward the alarm call just as the assigned squad cleared and said the building was secure—"False alarm." I kept going to the address. My partner started bitching at me, but I drove over anyway. My limited experience with the two other officers handling the call told me they were unlikely to get out of their car to check the doors of the building. When I looked down the t-alley behind the business, there was a trail of fishing tackle as far as I could see. Apparently it was not a false alarm.

My partner got on the radio asking for backup while I located the point of entry over a tin alley roof. The burglars had kicked out a small window on the second floor. I climbed up the clay drain spout, crawled through the broken window, and worked my way to the back door. What a surprise when I got downstairs and the entire shift, minus the sergeant and lieutenant, was waiting at the door. They poured in, grabbed paper bags, and began filling them up with fishing lures and other tackle. I started to say something but my partner for the day, a senior officer of the shift, told me to go to the office and call the owner so he could come down, and, "Oh, by the way, since you were so eager to get to this call, you do the report."

The cops were gone almost as quickly as the first set of burglars.

The owner showed up and we walked through the store together. He looked around for a few minutes, gave me a strange smile, and said he would have to make a list of missing goods.

> The NCIS (Britain's National Criminal Intelligence Service) minutes state that "common activities" of corrupt officers include theft of property. . . . (Seed, Palmer, September 27, 1998)

I got the necessary information to make a report and my partner drove me back to the precinct, complaining all the way back about how that "Old Jew" was going to inflate his burglary report to make a profit on the burglary. My guts were so tied up in knots I couldn't even respond. At the courthouse we parked outside and I started to get out of the car when my partner handed me a paper bag filled with fishing tackle. He said, "I know you like to fish. Here is your stuff."

I politely declined and he grabbed my arm and said, "You don't understand. This is the stuff you took." I knew what to do here. Since my luck going to sergeants had not been too good, I took the bag and was going straight to the lieutenant. This was burglary committed by cops! He needed to know immediately what was going on. But as I walked into the hallway to his office, I could hear the sergeant telling the lieutenant what good stuff the guys had picked up for him at the warehouse burglary.

I peeked in to see them sorting out *their* stuff in two bags on the lieutenant's desk. So much for telling anyone. I did the report, lies and all. Then I threw *my* bag of stuff in my locker so my partner could see and never said another word about it. Later on, I threw away the tackle. I never responded to another burglary or open door with those guys again.

I knew my regular partners were as honest as they come, though I had to admit I was disappointed they hadn't warned me about the other officers. But that is the insidious nature of the Code. It keeps even good officers from telling their rookies what is going on. In some ways it is a *rite of passage.* They want to see what you will do when you are exposed to it. I asked them what I should do.

My prior experience with the training sergeant showed me the consequences of reporting police misconduct. I knew no matter what I said in this case it would be denied at every level up through the lieutenant. They gave me good advice. "Stay away from those guys on their calls. They know how you feel now and will probably try very hard to not let you see them in action again."

I took my partners' advice and I never saw any of the other cops steal again. When I responded to burglaries or unsecured businesses, the other cops seldom stayed at the scene. There was that message again; if just one cop—even a rookie—says, "I'm not playing that game," the Code of Silence has no power.

> VICTORIA, AUSTRALIA—Police face criminal charges. More than 50 Victorian police have been suspended, forced to take leave or transferred while being investigated for a range of serious offences—a record number in the history of the force. Police have been stood down after

being charged with offences including rape, drug trafficking, burglary, and conspiracy to pervert the course of justice. Three have been suspended for shoplifting. (Silvester, February 17, 2003)

THERE ARE WORSE THINGS THAN THIEVES

The *Washington Post* reports two dozen officers face charges ranging from attempted murder, assault, grand larceny and drunken driving. (Fahrenthold, October 26, 2003)

I worked downtown Minneapolis for about nine years. One night, after bar closing, my partner and I were walking our beat when we found a badly beaten prostitute sitting propped up against a commercial dumpster. I knew this woman, but it took me a minute to recognize her. There was blood running from her mouth and nose, and her face was turning black and blue. Her jaw appeared to be broken from the angle it was at, and she was having trouble breathing. Unable to get her to her feet, we called for an ambulance and questioned her about what happened. Evasive and angry, she eventually said, "It was two cops."

I knew there were some cops who thought a good thumping was more effective than a trip to jail but I never actually saw anyone do it and I had never heard a cop accused of assault. Although she did reveal her assailants, she refused to make a report saying they'd told her, "If you ever snitch us off, we will kill you."

These two cops were known for their brutality on the street. My partner immediately told me he wanted "nothing to do with it" and "she refused to say who beat her up." He reminded me that this was "a whore who routinely robbed her tricks" and, in fact, as far as he was concerned, that's what happened. "Only this time she robbed the wrong guy and paid for it!" I was really disappointed in my partner. He was a good cop and an honest man, but he was going to stick to the Code for two guys he knew were brutal and dishonest because he knew everyone would cover for them.

He lectured me not to snitch on these two guys because they were protected, and dangerous. I took some time to think about this one and decided to go along because it had been a couple years since I'd drawn any heat from other cops, and I kind of liked it that way—at least for now.

A few days later my lieutenant asked me to join him and the deputy chief of police for lunch in a place known for its nighttime drug dealing. I had been thinking a lot about the hooker and the allegation she made about the two cops. Halfway through our meal I laid out the whole story. The deputy chief did not even raise an eyebrow.

My lieutenant, on the other hand, was sitting across the table from me going through visible contortions trying to get me to stop talking. But I continued and, when I was finished, the deputy chief looked me in the eye and said, "It was right to bring this to me. Have you told anyone else?" I told him, "No," and that my partner was no help either. He said, "That's OK, I'll take care of it." That magic, loaded phrase. It should have been a tip to me.

Two nights later I was walking through the courthouse, in uniform. One of the officers I had accused of assault grabbed me by the front of my jacket and pushed me into a corner. With his face touching mine he whispered with nearly fatal halitosis, "If you ever snitch us off again I will kill you." Then he walked away. The admission in his statement was both chilling and telling. He didn't say "accuse me," he said "snitch us off"—the same threat he'd used with the prostitute, and I believed him.

My head was spinning. The thought that I could be killed or have a *serious accident* as a result of telling the truth about rotten cops was a learning experience I was getting real tired of relearning. But then something positive happened. There were no more beatings of prostitutes in our district. There's no way to prove it, and I know there were other dynamics at work in this scenario, but it seemed like once again it only took one cop to say, "I'm not playing," and it stopped. The Code cannot operate in the face of truth.

> West New York Police Chief Alexander V. Oriente was sentenced to four years in state prison for his leading a band of rogue police officers in a ring of corruption. Prosecutors say from 1989 to 1997 his department took hundreds of thousands of dollars in bribes and kickbacks to protect prostitutes, illicit liquor sales, and illegal gambling operations. (Associated Press, January 5, 2000)

THE ADRENALINE FIX

Spring of 1994. It's 3 am and I'm pushing the limits of my squad, my luck—and the laws of physics—to reach officers in a foot chase with an armed and dangerous gang member. An attempted arrest gone bad—uniformed cops are trying to apprehend an armed and dangerous teenage gang member. You can hear the breathless cops gasping out directions as they run through yards and down alleys. I'm an adrenaline junky and I am getting a big fix tonight. This is what I live for; chasing bad guys with guns in the dark. My mind is fighting for control over my body as the adrenaline charges through me like an illegal drug.

It takes incredible effort and feels superhuman. My reflexes are faster and my pain tolerance is exponentially enhanced. It gives me an edge and a focus I feel in only one other activity. It's like great sex—and just as addicting.

In a foot chase, the odds always favor the bad guys. All they have to do is sit tight and wait until you get close and BANG— you're dead. And all too often that is exactly what happens, but not tonight. Our bad guy ran into a private home and the cops followed but couldn't find him. As I enter the house I hear cops screaming commands. When I turn on the single light bulb in the kitchen, I am greeted by the familiar and unnerving sound of an army of cock- roaches racing for the safety of darkness across a cheap suspended ceiling. I move quickly to the next room.

I finish searching the first floor with the officers who started the chase. As we get to the second floor I see my partner, another sergeant, punching the handcuffed home owner in the guts—our one potential witness. Nineteen years as a cop and once again I am witnessing a normally smart cop doing something that could end his career and put him in prison. I'm too far away at first to hear what is being said but I can see well enough down the hallway. My partner has this guy backed against a wall. As I start toward them my partner sees me and his half-completed punch turns into a grab of the guy's shirt.

There are usually two reasons why cops overreact like this, fear that leads to an overload of adrenaline, or stupidity, and this cop isn't stupid. Prior to this he had shown incredible bravery in facing armed and dangerous suspects and I know he would never tolerate one of the officers on our shift punching someone in handcuffs. I am left to believe the adrenaline got to him. It happens.

> Self-control is crucial for those in law enforcement. When facing someone who is in the throes of an amygdala hijack, like the abusive motorist, the odds of the encounter ending in violence will escalate rapidly if the officer involved gets hijacked by the amygdala, too. (Goleman 1995, 87).

As I got closer I could see my boss, our lieutenant, standing next to him. "What's going on?" I ask. They respond with silence. This is my first look at the home owner, an older black man. A full head taller than my partner, he is drooling drunk and howling obscenities as tears run down his face. I want to know how badly he is hurt, but I have more immediate concerns. We need to find our bad guy. A young officer, who also works for me on the Emergency Response Unit, says the house is clear. According to a witness he located and talked to, we chased the bad guy in one door and out the other.

I turn back and look at my partner. Without another word he takes the cuffs off the home owner and mumbles some sort of apology, his hands still shaking. I was right—too much adrenaline. We didn't catch our gang-banger that night, and two years later he shot and killed an eleven-year-old innocent in a drive-by shooting.

> THREE INDICTED IN '96 SLAYING OF BYRON PHILLIPS.
> A Hennepin County grand jury Tuesday indicted three Bogus Boyz gang members who were arrested in May for their role in the death of Byron Phillips, an 11-year-old Minneapolis boy hit by a stray bullet intended for a rival gang member.
>   The alleged shooters, Kawaskii A. Blanche, 24, and Montay A. Bernard, 25, were indicted on charges of first- and second-degree murder, conspiracy to commit murder and crimes committed for the benefit of a gang.
> (David Chanen, July 1, 1998, *Minneapolis Star Tribune*)

I still second guess our efforts from that night. If we had caught this guy with a gun that night, would that child be dead? If we had continued through the house and not stopped to rough up the homeowner would we have caught our bad guy?

I had some words with my partner and the lieutenant. I made it clear that if the old man complained, I would tell what I saw. But he didn't so I didn't.

As cops, we have all been guilty at one time or another of *little lies* or excessive force and the other cops never said a word to anyone. And many of us believe we owe our jobs to the fact that, when we screwed up, other cops showed us a way out through the Code. Unless the motivation is extremely powerful—like being sent to prison—cops don't tell on other cops.

> The fear of being labeled a "rat" and subsequently divorced from police culture has a seemingly powerful, negative impact on reporting corruption. This reveals a whole new dimension to the code of silence: it does not always reflect solely tolerance for corruption or a misplaced group loyalty. In many instances it is motivated purely by self-protection: a fear of the consequence of breaking the norms of loyalty and silence. (Mollen 1994, 56)

EVEN THE BEST TRAINING IS NOT ENOUGH

My own experience with the Code taught me that police departments don't suddenly get ethical because they have a new chief or new rules. But I saw positive changes occur in police behavior when new cops, fresh out of training, wouldn't tolerate some of the old ways. And I think that is even truer today. The rigorous psych exams, the detailed backgrounds and higher standards make it possible for agencies to hire people that are better suited to the job.

But with smarter and better trained cops, we also get cops who are smarter and better at using the Code of Silence. And some of the new cops I saw were very, very good at it. As a street supervisor, I saw how the new cops were being seduced by the Code. I became convinced I could make a difference if I could help prepare them for the ethical battles they were going to face in their own "walk with the devil." I wanted to be at the academy as a trainer.

I was assigned to the position of Police Academy Supervisor in the summer of 1994 and stayed there until spring of 1999 when I retired. In that short time period we trained about 300 new cops. In fact, by 1998 the majority of the street cops in Minneapolis had gone through my academy. I say "my" academy because I took immense pride in the staff and the job we did with recruits. I knew our training wasn't perfect, but I knew that what we were doing was making a difference. I didn't know the full impact until 1998 when I responded to a survey conducted by a reporter from Prince George's County, Maryland.

She was looking into the nature of police complaints and wanted some statistical data about Minneapolis. After gathering all the necessary information from our Internal Affairs Unit and the Civilian Review Authority, I called her with the numbers. She told me Minneapolis was the only major city in the U.S. at that point where the majority of the complaints were being made about officers with more than 5 years of service. This was amazing to her and me. I knew the academy couldn't claim sole responsibility for the decrease in complaints about new officers. But I knew in my heart something we were doing at the academy was working really well.

Then things started to go south. Complaints increased and recruits that went on ride-alongs with squads reported egregious conduct on the part of street cops. Some rogue cops didn't even care if their supervisors knew what they were doing. I'm sure that in some cases supervisors knew full well what was happening. But since it was only happening to "bad guys," they ignored it. Our field training program was failing, badly. Training officers would brag about using "creative report writing" to fill in the blanks when they didn't have any real probable cause, and the Code was protecting them all. Worst of all, the good cops, many of whom I had trained, were doing nothing to stop it. As good as our training was, I had missed something. That something was training new cops how to fight against the Code.

> There is a tragic irony to the code of silence which provides both the greatest challenge—and hope—in combating corruption. Although most honest cops will not report serious corruption, we despise corrupt cops and silently hope that they will be removed from the ranks. (Mollen 1994, 56)

A Day in the Life

WHAT DID YOU DO TODAY, DADDY?

POLICING IS CHALLENGING, exciting and rewarding, and cops don't always use the Code. Most of us just try to get our job done honestly and fairly and go home to our families. But there are duty shifts when it's so crazy from beginning to end we are tempted to do whatever it takes, including the Code, just to get through our shift. Take a typical night when things are really busy.

There are lots of calls for service. Most cars are an hour or more behind in getting to their assigned calls. Now I am waiting in the drive-up lane at the local fast food restaurant; there isn't time to sit down and eat a real meal. As I pull up to the pickup window there is a call for "officer needs help" a block away. I hit the lights and siren, stomp on the gas pedal and with a hard cut to the right I grind the squad over the cement divider and down the exit lane, tires squealing and burning onto the street. I reach the officers in seconds—with a serious leak from a damaged transmission pan.

I see a really big man up against the wall of the corner photo shop. He has an officer dangling from each arm. I can't tell who has a hold of whom. He is shaking them like rag dolls. I run from the squad and, stepping on the back of his left calf, I jump up, wrap my left arm around his neck as I make a fist with my right hand. I drive my right thumb into a pressure point just below his right ear and he collapses on the ground beneath me. I maintain the neck restraint while I press my forehead into the back of his wet and slippery head to keep him immobilized. The officers handcuff him, and then we slide him into their squad car head first.

I step out into the street light and realize I am covered in blood from my forehead to my gun belt. I can taste it and immediately start to get sick thinking of every ugly possibility. As I try to get most of the blood off my face with diaper wipes the senior officer tells me what happened.

The officers walked into the gas station to pay for their gas and this guy starts screaming and sweeping the shelves with his arms throwing everything on the floor. When they approached him he got even wilder, and they ended up chasing him to where I caught up with them. He pauses and I look at the rookie officer. The rookie avoids my eyes by looking at the ground. Not a good sign. The senior officer continues saying, "I hit him several times on the back of the head with my flashlight in an attempt to knock him down, but he only got wilder." I know I am not getting the full story, but it's clear I won't get any information out of the guy in the back of the squad, and it's just as clear that the rookie is going to stand by the training officer's story. I remind them to get all the details into the report and I leave. The Code was at work. I run home to change clothes, and I am back on the street in thirty minutes. The fast food joint is closed, but it doesn't matter. My stomach is too queasy to think about food now.

There are four drive-by shooting calls in the next hour. The same car is described in each one. Finally, one of the squads on my shift spots the car with multiple occupants and they make the stop. I am the second car on the scene. As I drive up, I can see there are several people in the car. Once I am in position behind my squad, I rack a round in the 12-gauge. The squad making the stop uses their pa system to talk the suspects out of the car. They direct the first passenger back to us where we have cover behind the squad cars.

The suspect, in his gang colors, is visibly agitated. Several times he reaches toward his waistband and starts to turn toward us. The shotgun aimed directly at his chest convinces him to put his hands in the air as he backs toward us. Other squads arrive. When the suspect reaches us, an officer takes control of him and immediately finds a loaded .38-caliber pistol in his waistband. He removes it, but, as soon as he takes his hands off the suspect, the suspect brings his arms down and reaches into his waistband. The officer grabs him in a bear hug from behind holding onto his hands. He yells that the guy has another gun in his hand. Now we are fighting for our lives. Several officers immediately step in to help.

In the struggle for control of the gun, the suspect sustains injuries to his shoulders, arms, torso, and neck. A rookie officer gets carried away in his use of force. It's his first felony stop with armed suspects. The bad guy is handcuffed, searched, and stuffed in the rear of a squad. Suspect #2 comes out of the car, and by now four other squads have responded. We have eleven adrenaline-charged officers pointing weapons at him as he walks back to us. He has a loaded semi-automatic pistol in his coat pocket. He is shaking with fear and secured without incident.

Two more suspects are taken out of the car, and the other squads transport them all to jail. Before I can leave, a citizen approaches and wants to make a complaint about the brutality she witnessed when we "choked and beat" the man we arrested. I assure her that we did only what was necessary. Not entirely true, but I am not going to take an excessive force complaint about a guy that just tried to kill us. I'll "walk with the devil" on this one, but I also make a mental note to talk to the rookie about his use of force.

According to the Victim Survey (NCVS), in 2009

- An offender was armed with a gun, knife, or other object used as a weapon in an estimated 22% of all incidents of violent crime.
- Offenders used firearms to commit 8% of violent crime incidents in 2009.
- Robberies (47%) were the most likely crime to involve an armed offender.
- Firearms (28%) were the most common weapons used in robberies.
- Most rapes and assaults did not involve the use of a weapon.
- From 1993–1997, of serious nonfatal violent victimizations, 28% were committed with a firearm, 4% were

committed with a firearm and resulted in injury, and less than 1% resulted in gunshot wounds. [4]

At the courthouse, I dictate my statement and get back on the street. My adrenaline has peaked and bottomed out twice already this shift, and I still haven't had any dinner. My stomach is starting to eat itself. I have to put something in there, soon. As I start toward a local all-night café, I get flagged down by a citizen in a bus stop. Thirty seconds later I am wrestling with a wino who hasn't bathed in at least six months. There are visible bugs on his neck and in his dirty matted beard.

> Body lice are small flattened insects with a slightly elongated body, lobed abdomen, a distinct head, small eyes, a pair of short antennae, and six legs, each terminating in a strong claw. Each of these stout claws has a small thumb-like spine for grasping, enabling the louse to move quickly around the clothes utilizing the fibers of the fabric or body hair for support. Adult lice are 2–4 mm in length, grey in color, but redden after blood feeding. (Dept. of Entomology, USYD Australia)

This old, homeless drunk has just assaulted a senior citizen in the bus shelter because she refused to give him a dollar. I handcuff him and search him, peeling back layer after layer of rotting clothing. The odor is strong enough that people 25 feet downwind are gagging. But I have to do it. I need to be sure he doesn't have any weapons. These old-timers often carry knives, and sometimes guns, for self-defense, and he is going in the back seat of my squad. He smells worse than a week-old DOA, and even with my iron gut, I begin to choke and gag on the smell.

Putting my hands into pockets that store this guy's *little treasures* completely creeps me out. I get the job done, but I am no longer hungry. I feel dirty and itchy the rest of the night. Not only that, but the jailers are angry with me for bringing him to jail and not the county detox. I complete the paperwork, drop off the squad to get it deloused, and pick up a spare squad. As I pull out of the police garage a car swerves completely across the street from the oncoming lanes and nearly hits me. I make a hard U-turn, hit the lights, and stop her in the next block. I can smell the alcohol coming from her car as she rolls down her window. As a matter of record, I ask if she has been drinking, and her response is, "All God damn day!" She is a smiling and cheerful thirty-something and wants to know why I stopped her, and if I'm single. There is a two-year-old baby sleeping on the back seat. I am on overtime when I finish this one.

That night as I lay next to my wife, I imagine I can feel bugs itching and crawling all over me. I wake up repeatedly, jerking and twitching from bad dreams about hepatitis, HIV, and other yet-to-be-named blood borne pathogens from the guy with the split open head. About 3 am the phone rings. It's the on-duty watch commander, and he tells me, "Great job on shooters in the car. Guns were stolen. Probably get a commendation. The problem is the guy whose blood you "shared" had to be admitted to the hospital.

You need to get down to the hospital right away in the am for your gamma glob shots and blood work. Now get some sleep."

Injections of gamma globulin are used to create a rapid but temporary immunity in patients who have been exposed to certain diseases.

Now I am wide awake wondering, "Where is my bloody uniform? Did my wife touch it? Did my children touch it? I go to the laundry and find the uniform shirt in the washer." I pull it out. It's ruined from the blood. "Shit, $35 down the drain. I didn't need that." As I fall asleep my final thought is. "I wonder if the Air Force will take me back."

IT ALL STARTS HERE

Most people start in policing because they want to help people. But the Code of Silence sets many traps for the new cop. The *bait* is often a simple mistake. In fact, a new cop makes many mistakes, and even veteran officers occasionally trip up. When that happens, training officers will often take the opportunity to indoctrinate a new officer into the Code. A good example is the inappropriate use of force. Assuming it was not intentional, this is a mistake most of us make when we are learning to wield our new-found power.

Consider the typical arrest and handcuffing of a drunk, a compliant person who suddenly decides they are not going to jail. Training provides that we put the person in a specific posture, then position ourselves to safely handcuff them. In the case of a compliant, non-aggressive, and sober person this works well, but there are also a lot of people who resist. The behavior that leads to an arrest usually involves alcohol or drugs, and some sort of physical act requiring the police to intervene. The thought of going to jail is just an added inducement for some to resist arrest. Another problem is that people going to jail seem to know when the officer is new on the job.

The nervousness, the hesitant manner and constant looking to the partner for approval all announce ROOKIE! Even so, the rookie officer is always anxious to arrest someone and no crime is too small to go unenforced. Put yourself in this rookie's shoes.

You are on foot patrol in a downtown alley with your training officer when you observe a young woman urinating in the alley behind a bar. She is in full view of a group of well-dressed theater goers. With their noses in the air they, who expect to be obeyed, tell you to, "Do something!"

As you approach her, she stands and staggers a little. Her speech is slurred as she explains (in one breath) that there was a line in the bar for the women's can and she was about to piss her pants she didn't know she could be seen from the street she was in such a hurry to pee and "those assholes in the men's room" wouldn't let her use a stall and now she's pissed all over her new shoes because you surprised her and made her jump and . . .

You interrupt her ramblings to ask for ID, but she left her purse with her friends in the bar. You know the bar is hostile to cops, and your partner is quick to say, "We are not going in there to get her ID." You assume the only option is arrest. It never occurs to you to just let her go. You tell her she is under arrest for urinating in public. You put your hands on her and turn her around to handcuff her. She begins to struggle and call you names. This is not a fight, just active resistance, but her arms are wet and slick with sweat, and you are quickly losing control.

Statistics and your officer survival training have drilled into you that any struggle that lasts more a minute usually results in an escalated use of force and injuries to either the officer or the person being arrested. From your training you also know that some drunks don't even realize they are causing a problem for the officer. About three seconds have passed, and she is pulling away. You need to respond. You use a tactic that takes her to the ground quickly so you can handcuff her, but it puts her face into a broken bottle you did not see in the dark. When you turn her over there is a large laceration across her cheek, and through her nose and it is pouring blood. You are momentarily stunned by what you see, and *your partner's only comment is, "What the fuck did you just do!"*

You used the training you received and things have gone very badly. She is still resisting and now your partner has stepped in to help control her. Blood is going everywhere, and you are trying to call for an ambulance and control her at the same time. The blood makes her hands and arms extremely slippery, and you have to use additional pressure to hold on to her, which causes additional bruising and more screamed obscenities.

As my partner Roy used to say, "Once again we have snatched defeat from the jaws of victory."

About this time the bar empties out into the alley. When they see you "beating" this badly bloodied woman they become hostile and threatening. You and your partner drag her, kicking and screaming, out to the street and quickly get her into the arriving ambulance. In the process she loses her shoes and gets abrasions on her heels. You tear her slacks in the struggle, and one breast is now hanging out of her torn tank top. You get her in the ambulance as quickly as possible and tell the medics to get moving.

As the junior officer you ride to the hospital with her and listen to her constant 100-decibel tirade about the "fuckin cops." Then, just as you get to the hospital she turns to you and says, "Officer, thank God you're here. Some cops beat me up in the alley. Look what they did to me!" All you can do is stare in silence. She doesn't have a clue what happened.

You are covered in her blood from the struggle. It is all over your shirt and face. You can taste it, and that's not a good thing. The medic is advising you to wash it off as best you can with the wipes he is handing you. You start thinking about the blood borne pathogen lecture on HIV/AIDS and hepatitis, and your stomach is turning. Things have gone badly because in your eagerness to do your job, and your lack of experience, you didn't consider other options to arrest or physical force. And, although you employed the tactic correctly, you probably should have used a different takedown in this location with this woman.

You have a very petty crime, and a very major injury which you have to believe will result in a very major lawsuit. You are still on probation, and your use of force will probably be viewed as unreasonable in light of the injuries sustained by the young woman. As a rookie, you could lose your job. Your career in law enforcement will be over before it begins. Trust me—this is exactly what's going through your mind.

Your partner, a senior officer, also knows that when this woman complains and you go to internal affairs and admit you disfigured her face in the process of handcuffing her, when she wasn't really fighting back, while being arrested for a crime for which you could have just as easily let her go, you will both be named in the inevitable lawsuit and some attorney will make a lot of money.

In a best case scenario you see days off without pay and your name in the paper being accused of maiming an innocent young woman with no prior record. A zero chance of promotion or ability to transfer to a specialty unit is all in your future, if you can call it that. And, best of all, when your senior partner shows up at the hospital, she brings up each and every one of these possibilities to make sure you understand the gravity of the situation for both of you. Your partner knows from years of experience how to push a person's buttons, and now she's pushing yours.

She reminds you, "Remember what happened to the cops in the Rodney King case? Can you say 'Hi, I'm your new cellmate?' What do you think this young woman's face will look like on the 10 o'clock news, especially when they do a side-by-side comparison with her virginal pre-tattoo and metal-free junior prom photos? The pictures will be gory and sensational closeups, and they will be on the evening news for about a week. With every complaint of excessive force you get from this day forward, those pictures will resurface in the news."

After running all these possibilities by you, she lets you stew in silence for a short while. She says she better do the paperwork on the arrest while you sit at the hospital with the prisoner. You really have no choice, as junior officer you do what the senior officer says. Her final words to you at the hospital are, "Do not under any circumstances say anything other than she was fighting with us and fell on some broken glass. Have you got that?" You get it all right. You are already considering other career options, if you don't end up in prison.

While waiting with your prisoner in the emergency room, you suffer the wrath of the ER nurses. You note that they are getting their own story from her, in between her sobs and tears, about what happened. They take lots, and lots, of pictures of the wound, her clothing, and her bruises. The nurse's questions to you are thinly veiled investigations into what you did to this young woman. They will see, once you get the blood washed off, that you do not have a single scratch. A nurse with a mocking smile will casually list for you all the potentially devastating diseases you may have been exposed to from the prisoner's blood, based on the needle tracks on her arms and her history of hepatitis, herpes, gonorrhea, and an HIV-positive boyfriend. Her final question to you is, "Did you hit her in the abdomen area? I need to know. She's pregnant."

> Hepatitis C is a virus that causes inflammation of the liver resulting in liver damage that can lead to cirrhosis, cancer, and death. HCV's rapid genetic changes allow this virus

to avoid a host immune response; therefore greater than 85 percent of people infected with this virus develop chronic hcv infection. One of the risk factors for HCV infection—*contact with infected blood.*
(Texas Department of Health)

It doesn't take long before you really dislike the ER staff and your prisoner. In the meantime a number of her drunk and angry friends from the bar have shown up at the hospital, and they are very hostile. They start threatening you with lawsuits and other unnatural and unspeakable acts of violence. Hospital security eventually takes them away. You begin to wonder if your partner abandoned you and went home.

Now the watch commander, the chief's representative, shows up at the hospital. He takes one look at your prisoner and says, "Your report will be in my hands before you go home tonight, officer."

After an eternity of two hours, your partner gets back to the hospital with the report. She tells you to issue a citation and leave it with the young woman now that she is sobering up and waiting for the plastic surgeon. "You know the rules. If you make 'em bleed, you got to arrest 'em for something, and we can't take her to jail at this point," she says. "I ran her name and birthdate and she comes up clear warrants, living at the address she gave us. Besides, it's time for dinner and I need to change shirts and get some coffee before you get us into any more shit tonight."

First stop is the station to shower and change clothes. Worried, angry, and dejected, you go to dinner with your partner where you meet with two other veteran cops from the precinct. As you all sit down the senior partner gives you a copy of the two-page arrest report detailing the crime and the officer's actions.

It reads in part: "Responding to a citizen's complaint about a female urinating in public, officers encountered an angry drunk with her pants down urinating in the alley. When told she was under arrest, she swung at the officers with her fists and tried to kick Officer Smith in the testicles. Off balance when her kick was deflected by the officer's quick actions, she fell. Officer Smith tried to catch her before she hit the ground.

The officer's attempts were in vain, and the young woman hit her face on the ground landing on a broken liquor bottle that could not be seen in the dark. She responded violently and it took both officers to handcuff her. After handcuffing her, Officer Smith provided first aid and the prisoner was immediately transported by ambulance to the hospital for treatment in the emergency room. Neither officer was injured in the arrest. Prisoner was tagged in lieu of arrest and left in the care of the hospital."

You don't know what to think. Clearly this is not what happened. There was struggle, that's true, and you did provide first aid, but you don't remember her trying to kick you or swinging at you. The Code has surfaced. Your senior partner passes the report to the other veteran officers and they voice their unanimous approval with comments like, "It's a God damn work of art, as usual. You are lucky, kid, that you have her as a partner."

When you start to question what will happen if anyone finds out the truth, all three senior officers are quick to give advice.

"Kid, it's on paper, so this is the truth. You didn't do anything wrong. That's what happens when you use all that Kung Fui shit you learned at the academy. You took her down, and it was just bad luck this stupid bitch got hurt, but that's her fault, not yours. If you are one hundred percent truthful, do you think it would help? You will be up to your ass in internal affairs, the FBI, and civil suits. She was drunk, she won't remember what happened. You made a common rookie mistake. It's handled now, just don't let it become a habit."

The final word comes from your partner. "Listen. I did the paperwork. I witnessed the whole thing, and I am the only witness. Besides, everything is already filed and in the computer. I feel bad for this girl too, sort of, and the city will probably pay for her surgery, but if we don't stick together on this, your job and mine are on the line for something she caused, not us." She pauses.

"I am only doing this for you because you are a good kid and I know you want to do a good job. This is not the academy, this is the street. This is how it works. We haven't done anything wrong, and you know it! The bottom line is you don't have to do anything. If it goes to court, I'll testify and you won't have to do shit. I am doing you a huge favor here."

She pauses again and waits for her words to sink in. "Do you want me to tell the truth? Do you want me to say 'my rookie partner overreacted and without consulting me on options threw the prisoner into broken glass as he took her to the ground?' Is that what you want?"

She sits back and slowly finishes her coffee, letting you consider the options. "Have you got your next job interview lines memorized, 'Welcome to Burger World, may I take your order?' Is that what you want to do next? Well, it wouldn't really matter if that was what you wanted. Cops don't do that to other cops. We all make mistakes out here. It's that kind of job. Shit, you weren't even angry, and you told her she was under arrest when you took her down. Just wait till you lose your temper and someone gets hurt. What are you going to do then? Run to IA and confess that you lost control and just fucked them up cause you were pissed? It doesn't work like that, and you know it. Now let's get back to work and arrest some real bad guys for a change. And remember this—we are the only ones out here in the real world who will be there for you, and *we take care of our own.*"

And so it begins: they covered for you, and now you are expected to cover for them. If you keep your mouth shut, you will pass your first "test," acceptance of the Code over the truth.

> As testimony at the Commission's public and private hearings made clear, supervising officers tip off subordinates about pending investigations or citizen complaints. On some occasions, desk officers reminded officers to add resisting arrest charges for suspects brought to the stationhouse with too many visible bruises. (Mollen 1994, 64)

COMMITTED TO THE TRUTH

But what if you want to tell the truth? What are your options here? Go to your supervisor and say the senior officer lied on her report? I can tell you from experience that almost never works. It's just your word against hers, and you're the one who caused all the injuries. Your partner came to your rescue after you screwed things up. She's willing to help you out of a jam. Now you're going to rat on her? Are you going to give up policing over this one incident? I ask only because if you go to IA and complain about her for something like this, other cops will make your life so miserable you will probably quit. There are other problems, too. Once you've snitched off a cop that tried to help you, especially a respected senior officer, you are a pariah. So options within the department are limited.

> Honest officers who know about or suspect corruption among their colleagues, therefore, face an exasperating dilemma. We perceive that we must either turn a blind eye to the corruption we deplore, or risk the dreadful consequences of reporting it. The commission's inquiries reveal that the overwhelming majority of officers choose to live with the corruption. (Mollen 1994, 57)

But there is something you can do for yourself to satisfy the dilemma. You can learn from this mistake and vow to not make it again. You can recommit yourself to being truthful—that you will never let another lie go into one of your reports. I don't mean promising you will never use inappropriate force again. It's almost impossible to use just the right amount of force every time someone resists. I am talking about making a commitment to the truth.

So, let's say you do that. The city attorney has declined to prosecute. You won't have to perjure yourself in court, and you're feeling a little better about everything. After a few weeks, you look back on the arrest as a do-over. But just when you think you have the answer, you get blindsided. You are sued for violating her civil rights, excessive force, unlawful arrest, etc., and now you have to give a sworn deposition about what happened. Now what?

Where is your commitment to the truth now? Do you abide by the Code, or do you tell the truth. If you do tell the truth at this point, you could lose your job. At the very least, you will lose all credibility with the courts and the cops.

In the meantime, the local newspaper has reported the lawsuit. Just as your partner predicted, there are the pictures of a sweet innocent prom queen next to the ER photos. The woman's attorney is demanding a list of all your goods, bank accounts, pension funds, stocks, your boat, your cabin, and other worldly possessions. Your whole life is reduced to a list of what you will lose if the suit is successful. And now your wife and family are part of the deal. The kids are being taunted at school, and the people your wife works with are asking her all sorts of totally inappropriate personal questions. You've hired an attorney on your credit card, and you can feel your whole life swirling around in the lawsuit toilet, just before the flush.

Your partner is sticking to her story no matter what, so you no longer see telling the truth as an option. She won't even talk about other ways out of this, and the rest of the cops on the shift are making sure you understand what happens to cops who snitch on other cops. So you stick with the lie and, although your testimony is terrible, and you're sure they know you are lying, they find you not guilty. Or, even better, the department decides to settle the case before it goes to the jury and you are finally off the hook.

You still have your job, your senior partner now trusts you because you lied to cover for her lies, and everything is cool. Right? Maybe, maybe not. Try answering the following questions:

Are you going to depend on the Code and lie the next time you make a mistake?

What are your options when your partner lies in her report?

What are your options when you are the only one in a group of officers who wants to tell the truth about a particular event?

For the rookie in this incident the senior officer created a trap, a catch-22 with no escape route. The rookie did everything correctly. It was just bad luck the injuries were so severe. An older, smarter officer would have just told the truth and defended the use of force. The city would have paid for some or all of the reconstructive surgery for the girl's face and that would have been that. But what about when there are no witnesses and you make a mistake? What are the costs of being truthful when you are the only one involved in the incident? What are you willing to do to maintain your integrity?

The Code of Silence is a zero-sum game. You can't have integrity and play the Code of Silence game because every time you use it to win the game of "convict and incarcerate" you lose honor and integrity. Sadly, a lot of the cops succumb to the Code. It becomes a way of doing business for them. And, try as you might, there will be times when you will do your own "walk with the devil." But you can decide, one instance at a time, to do it differently. You can say, "I'm not playing."

POLICE ACADEMY—THIS IS A TEST

In the Minneapolis police academy it was, and I assume still is, customary to have new recruits go on ride-alongs with officers. The real world exposure to policing helps the recruit better connect with the concepts being taught in the academy classroom. As the academy supervisor I required each recruit to tell the class how the officers they rode with responded to different calls. After one particular round of ride-alongs, my academy training partner and I were in the classroom listening to the recruits tell their tales. Their excitement was infectious and never failed to remind us of why we became cops. But, even with our combined experience of 40 years, we were not prepared for what happened to one recruit.

She was assigned to ride with a two-officer squad. Early in the shift they stopped a car with a black female driver. They could have arrested her, but after talking to her they gave her a break because she told them when and where a large quantity of crack cocaine was going to be delivered later that night. A couple of hours later the ride-along officers met with other officers from the precinct at a local diner and made plans to do a forcible entry into the house, assuming, correctly, that there would be guns. At the appointed time the squads took up their positions. The two officers in the ride-along car ran to the front door, forced it open, and took down everyone inside. They recovered a large quantity of crack cocaine and at least one weapon. It all sounded pretty exciting, but there were some details missing from her story that I wanted the rest of the class to hear, so I asked the logical question, "Who got the warrant for them to do the forced entry?"

The recruit, in all innocence and complete candor, said she had the same question because there was no warrant and no narcotics team involvement. She asked the officers where they got the probable cause to do a forced entry on the house so many hours after they received the information. Without hesitation and with much boasting, they told her it was "creative report writing." They would say they saw a hand-to-hand transfer of drugs in front of a known drug house and chased the suspect into the house in hot pursuit. "That's how it's done out here."

I told the entire class it was an unlawful entry and they were not to take this one example as the way police work is usually done in Minneapolis. We reviewed with the entire class the concepts of probable cause, exigent circumstances, and the importance of obtaining a warrant. I made it perfectly clear that this was not only unacceptable behavior, it was incredibly dangerous and criminal. I took the case to Internal Affairs, but I was made to look the fool when investigators cleared the officers of any wrong doing.

Consider the magnitude of this deception. Based on the cadet's description of the events, there were at least six officers involved in this warrantless entry. It was told to 20-plus people in complete candor. She had no agenda; no reason to make up even one part of the story, and yet, when I gave this information to Internal Affairs, the investigation was closed without interviewing me or any of the recruits present in the classroom. I asked if the suspect was interviewed, and I was told he was not. He was a drug dealer and "he pled guilty, why bother?"

> We found that police corruption cases were often closed prematurely, minimized, and fragmented into separate parts, which insured that the nature and extent of corruption uncovered would be minimal. The difficult issue was to determine whether this reflected a knowing cover up, simple incompetence, or both. (Mollen 1994, 59)

The recruit who told us about these rogue cops was staying with a Minneapolis police officer at the time. True to form, when she came in the next day she did not want to talk about it any further. I am sure she had been told in no uncertain terms what her honesty would cost her. Her introduction to the Code was brutal, and could have been career ending. When the two officers she rode with heard that she had reported the whole incident to the class, they began spreading rumors that she was a snitch, not to be trusted. We heard by way of the grapevine that they were bragging "She will never make it through her FTO (Field Training Program) period in our precinct."

We never heard a single rumor that these cops were accusing her of lying—just breaking the Code. This practice of kicking in doors without a warrant and then using the Code to cover for their acts was so ingrained it probably never even occurred to them to deny their actions to other cops. And they were willing to destroy this recruit's career because she had broken the Code of Silence regarding their criminal behavior before she even got on street. Of course, she wasn't the first and she won't be the last.

INTERNAL AFFAIRS

What can I say about IA? If they had gone forward and proven the complaint, which should not have been too difficult, the department would have been looking at another national scandal on the heels of a finding of "deliberate indifference" by the courts. Who knows what that would have cost the city? Was that a factor in IA's decision to not pursue the case? Maybe. It doesn't really matter. The cops on the street knew what really happened, and the message to them was very clear—IA and the Chief do not want the truth any more than cops want to tell it to them! They just want crack dealers arrested. IA could not have done a better job of reinforcing the Code if they tried. The message to the recruit class was disastrous: *the chief will say what he believes, but the truth is you can do whatever it takes to lock up drug dealers.*

There was nothing I could say or do to repair the damage done by this one incident. It took all meaning out of every ethics lecture the chief or academy staff had ever given. And as bad as that was, it wasn't the worst of it. This failure on the part of Internal Affairs and the administration to hold two rogue cops accountable for their illegal activities was a sucker punch delivered to every ethical, fair-minded cop in the department. It was a validation of every complaint the department had received about police abuse of authority, and we did it to ourselves in the name of the Code of Silence!

Here are excerpts from a March 2008, article from the *Portland Mercury News*.

THE THICK BLUE LINE
A former Portland cop is planning to sue the city over allegations she was effectively terminated in retaliation for "snitching" on an officer who was supposed to be training her. . . .

On May 23, 2007, [Officer Lindsay K.] Hunt was assigned to Northeast Precinct under a new training coach, Officer Quency Ho, after completing Portland's 16-week "Advanced Academy" training.

Hunt alleges that on May 24, 2007, she and Ho responded to a call regarding a potential altercation at a residence in the area of NE 60th and Sandy. Another officer was on the scene, and took the lead in talking to the neighbors who called the police, as well as to the suspect, who was alone in his ground-floor apartment watching television. Based on his conversations with the neighbors and with the cooperative suspect, the other officer found a lack of probable cause and thanked the suspect for his time, according to the tort claim.

"After the suspect shut his door," the claim continues, "Offer Ho began trying to kick the door down. Ms. Hunt stopped Officer Ho. Officer Ho then drew his firearm, walked to the side of the apartment to an open window, and, pointing his gun at the suspect, demanded he unlock the front door.

"As the suspect began unlocking the front door, Officer Ho forced open the door and attacked the suspect, slamming him against the wall and putting him in a choke hold," the tort claim says. "After roughing him up for a while, Officer Ho left. There was no legal basis for this action. Ms. Hunt demanded that Officer Ho stop his illegal activity, but was ignored.

"Despite Ms. Hunt's plea that Officer Ho refrain from needlessly beating up civilians and that Officer Ho, at the very least, needed to fill out a use-of-force report for drawing a firearm, Officer Ho responded, 'If no one finds out, we won't get caught. Look the other way,'" the claim continues. "Ms. Hunt was stunned by Officer Ho telling her to keep quiet about the incident. . . .

The tort claim makes several other allegations about Officer Ho, including that he took goods several times without payment from the 7-Eleven at NE Weidler and 3rd, and told Hunt to do the same. . . . He is also alleged to have told Hunt she was not "manly" enough to be a cop.

Hunt reported her concerns to the cops' training division but was allegedly told "you can have all the integrity you want in six months when you are no longer on probationary status if you keep your mouth shut," according to the tort claim.

Hunt also claims a training officer told her she was no longer physically safe and that if she ever needed backup, no Portland Police officer would respond because she was a "snitch. . . ." Following Hunt's allegedly coerced resignation, her reputation as a "snitch" is said to have spread quickly through the police bureau because of defamatory statements made by cops. . . .[5]

Early in my career I was assigned to Internal Affairs. One day I received a complaint from a paramedic with a long history of outstanding work. He said he'd called the cops for assistance because he had a mentally unstable patient who was threatening the paramedics. When the cops arrived, they had to wrestle with the guy to restrain him face down on a litter. One of the responding officers was a particularly big and strong man, but he was slightly injured in the scuffle and was angry about it.

He entered the ambulance just before it left the scene and punched the restrained mental patient in the face so hard he broke his jaw. The paramedic was angry with the cop and exchanged some heated words before he left the scene with the patient. When they got to the ER it was clear the jaw was broken, and the medic was put on the spot for what happened. Although he initially covered for the cops, he knew it was a lie. His conscience bothered him and he came in a couple of days later to make a statement. When I showed him the police report, he said, "That's not what happened."

When I interviewed the accused officer's partner, he claimed he was in the squad writing on the log sheet and didn't see anything.

So, we had a patient with a freshly broken jaw, a respected paramedic's first-hand account of the assault, a false police report, a Code-of-Silence-blind partner, but a victim that couldn't tell you what planet he lived on much less what happened to him. What were the chances of any real justice here? None. The chief's finding was "not sustained." It was blatant deceit and a serious break in trust with our paramedics at the hospital. I'm sure they concluded that cops are brutal, and as long as cops invoke the Code, *they* have the power. Now ask me again why the ER staff is so hard on cops when we bring in injured patients.

What's really telling is when you talk to the ER staff it is always the same officers bringing in patients to be treated after "resisting arrest." Why do you suppose that is? The answer is simple: they are using excessive force. Fortunately the majority of cops use only the force necessary to get the job done, and that seldom leads to the emergency room. But as long as only cops are investigating cops, the Code of Silence will usually prevail and the public will never get a true picture of what is going on in the street.

But the Code is not the only road block to justice in IA. Part of the problem comes from the way Internal Affairs is viewed by most cops. If you are looking to move up the ranks, then an assignment to IA is seen as a ticket punch on your promotion card. You do your time, try to not to hurt anyone, then get out as soon as you can. You will be investigating former partners, future bosses, past supervisors, and friends—the same people who covered for you when you made mistakes. You know and they know that a thorough investigation often means breaking the Code of Silence, and most cops are not going to do that.

The other problem is that it is very difficult to prosecute cops unless there is overwhelming evidence that includes the testimony of other cops, video/audio recordings, or other physical evidence. If it comes down to the accused cop's story vs. the complainant's story, the cop will usually be found not guilty. This can be true even when there is physical evidence to support a claim of misconduct. When the Code of Silence is invoked, and the cops stick together on their story, there is little hope of justice being served.

> Moreover, we found that IAD's investigative system reacted solely to isolated complaints. It did not pursue patterns of corruption and conspiratorial wrongdoing as was done in investigative commands other than IAD. Of course, such an approach guarantees that the full scope of corruption will never come to light. (Mollen 1994, 102)

The Narcotics Investigator

Power tends to corrupt and absolute power corrupts absolutely.

LORD ACTON, 1834–1902

UNDERCOVER WORK

NARCOTICS UNDERCOVER WORK is the assignment that most often seduces cops to "walk with the devil." The independence, lack of immediate supervision, and the need to get inside the heads of dope dealers are all part of narcotics investigations. To catch drug dealers, you have to act like a dealer or a user. It's hard to learn, and for some it's even harder to stop once they've learned it. On top of that, there is tremendous frustration within police ranks over the war on drugs and where it's going. Cops know we aren't winning and that police work alone is not going to stop gangs and drug use.

That's why research undertaken by Joseph McNamara, former police chief of San Jose, is especially startling. McNamara, now a research fellow at the conservative Hoover Institution at Stanford University, surveyed nearly 500 police chiefs, police officers, district attorneys, public defenders, lawyers, judges and Stanford students.

Except for the police, who hail from across the country, they live in Northern California.

He found that 95 percent of the police officers believed the United States was losing the war on drugs, and 98 percent thought drug abuse was not primarily a police problem. Just over 90 percent of the cops said increased prevention and treatment could control drugs more effectively. More than 30 percent of the cops said that legalization or decriminalization would cause a decrease in drug use or else not affect it. (*San Francisco Examiner,* April 9, 1995)

Cops have no influence or control over the root causes of crime like poverty or educational levels. So we exert our control where we can have the greatest effect—in the poor communities, where the violence surrounding drug dealing is most apparent. The conviction and incarceration of crack dealers and users becomes our number one priority. It is a win/win situation for cops who want a lot of action. Nobody likes drug dealers—not the citizens, not the cops, not the county attorney, not the politicians—and for good reason. At least 90 percent of crime is directly related to drug use. Besides, working crack dealers is exciting. They carry guns, usually stolen. They run, sometimes generating police chases. They are the most likely dirtbags to shoot at cops. That means they are the bad guys we are most likely to be able to shoot at. It doesn't get much better than that.

We learn this lesson early in our careers. When legal means aren't working and nobody expects us to address the causes of crime, even good cops will occasionally give in to the old "ends justify the means" sort of policing. Some will make it their goal in life to convict and incarcerate drug dealers. They will shake them down wherever and whenever. They go through their pockets, tear their cars apart, turn their houses upside down, and constantly harass them. Of course, many cops fail to remember that these guys don't usually own the homes being searched. Street level drug dealers often live with (off of) a girlfriend or family member. This was exemplified by a comment made to one of my old partners when she asked a drug dealer why he had such a nice car but no place to live.

He responded, "You can live in your car. You can't drive your house." Of course, there is more to it than that. An expensive car is a status symbol, a way to measure yourself against your competitors and peers. It proves you are somebody! What status does the community give to someone who can afford only an old house in a poor neighborhood? We all know the answer to that one.

My point is this. Rich or poor, good and bad people live in every neighborhood. Cops tend to forget that as they deal with only the criminals or victims. The result is that we marginalize neighborhoods and make assumptions about the people who live there. For example, in executing a very high profile "clean up the neighborhood" high-risk warrant, we broke down the back door of a beautiful home only to find a stone deaf, very old lady sitting on her couch watching TV. The crack dealers living next door had been using her front porch to sell drugs at night, without her knowledge. But the narcotics officers didn't bother to find that out until it was too late. It was considered a "drug infested" neighborhood.

The good news was she had a very rickety and drafty back door prior to our "arrival." Now she has a very secure and weather tight door—courtesy of the city! Of course you don't see these tactics being used in the affluent neighborhoods where the use of cocaine is open and almost flaunted. But then suburban drug users don't typically shoot at each other from behind their $500,000 homes, killing innocent children in their crossfire.

I'm not criticizing the cops who harass crack dealers. We should be working hardest where the most violence is occurring; that only makes sense. And we do recover guns and some drugs. But good undercover work and surveillance are a lot more productive. They're just a lot more difficult to plan, more labor intensive, and not as sexy as running up on dealers and shaking them down in front of the whole world. If you don't understand what I am talking about, watch the Spike Lee movie, *Clockers*. It shows exactly how street narcotics are dealt in poor neighborhoods and does an excellent job of depicting the police "jump out."

The deal and the jump out are in the very beginning of the movie. Officers roll up in their unmarked cars. Everyone within reach is taken to the ground or to a wall, searched for drugs and checked for warrants. Then they are let go after the requisite derogatory comments about their heritage. They don't find any drugs on the dealers, so they can't make any arrests.

Don't be concerned when you can't understand anything the street dealers are saying in the beginning of the show, you're not supposed to, it's street talk. Don't stop after the first scene. Watch the whole movie. This is an excellent depiction of the conflict between cops and dealers.

So how does the Code of Silence fit into all this? Seamlessly.

COPS ALREADY KNOW WHO'S GUILTY

If cops seldom actually catch anyone with drugs on them and we need to do that to make arrests, what will we do—besides illegally kick in doors without warrants?

Street dealers are smart, or they don't stay street dealers. They know we will search their mouths and their bodies thoroughly. They also know not to carry any more than two or three rocks of crack on them at any given time. If by chance they do get caught with a small amount, they can plead "personal use." They have also learned to keep it in their hand. They work the street from a vantage point that allows them at least a half a block to react to approaching cars. If they see a squad car coming, they can just drop the drugs and walk away. If they get stopped and searched, they don't have anything on them. If they are released, they can walk back and pick up the drugs later. Cops and dealers both know this is how it works.

The dealer will have the drugs in his hand until he sees the cops and then he drops them. As cops approach, the dealer will mark the spot where we first saw him. Often we will even see the dealer put one hand behind his back when we first spot him. We stop the dealer/suspect and then go to the spot we marked to look for the crack cocaine. If we find it, the report often reads "as officers approached the suspect, a known crack cocaine dealer, officers saw the suspect throw down small packages that were immediately recovered and tested positive as crack cocaine." Nobody questions the cops. A lot of the same dealers are caught repeatedly, so there is a lot of corroboration that the person being arrested is a crack dealer.

After tons of those arrests, we know the street dealer drops the drugs behind his back, even if we can't see it. Time and again it is proven to us when we find the drugs. But this flawed reasoning becomes a trap for cops. Pretty soon we find it easy to arrest people for crimes based on what we know, and we let creative report-writing fill in the blanks. It becomes a way of doing business.

> One commonly identified factor associated with drug-related corruption was a police culture that was characterized by a Code of Silence, unquestioned loyalty to other officers, and cynicism about the criminal justice system. Such characteristics were found not only to promote police corruption, but to impede efforts to control and detect it. (GAO, May 1998, 4)

MIXING THE TRUTH WITH SMALL LIES

Here's one example of just how institutionalized and pervasive the attitude of "knowing" has become. I was a member of the Emergency Response Unit from 1978 to 1994. By 1993, I was a command post supervisor for hostage and barricaded suspect operations. As a sergeant, I was also responsible for doing a month of high-risk warrant service at least twice and sometimes three times a year. In an assigned month, the team of five or six officers would execute anywhere from three to eleven high-risk warrants per day. Each warrant required reconnaissance, planning, the use of rams or barricade breeching munitions, and all the adrenaline you could muster for about ten minutes of incredibly high-stress work on each warrant.

The execution of the warrant is the end result for most cops. It all really begins days, months, or years earlier with the narcotics investigation. Narcotics officers will develop enough information to get a no-knock warrant for the location. That means the officers can make a forced entry without waiting for someone to open the door. We are allowed to do this when there is good reason to believe guns or other weapons are present, and the occupants of the location are likely to use them. It is a great tool in providing for officer safety. It takes only a few of these entries to realize how dangerous they are. The energy level and sense of threat are at an incredibly high level.

I led many warrants where we encountered people with guns in hand, ready to shoot, but there was enough "shock and awe" in our entry they never had a chance to use them.

In other cases, the first officer in the door, directly in front of me, made good decisions and did what needed to be done, not what he could have legally done. If those officers had acted just within the legal limits of the law, I can say there would have been at least six dead crack dealers in Minneapolis just from the high-risk warrants my team completed. But there aren't, because most cops don't work that way.

THE ENTRY

In addition to the 30+ pounds of equipment each officer wears as part of their regular uniform, the team is equipped with heavy body armor, automatic weapons, bullet-resistant shields, a very heavy ram for knocking down the door, and other tools as deemed necessary. Every officer going through the door is making a tremendous physical effort, in addition to the mental effort, to stay focused and not let high adrenaline levels take over. And it only gets worse once you get inside.

There may be from three to thirty or more people inside. Our job, with a team of just six officers, is to secure and handcuff every person in the house before anyone gets a chance to start shooting. The cops are yelling, "GET DOWN, GET DOWN!" The people inside are yelling and screaming, sometimes going for guns. There may be children running and screaming, babies lying on the floor, people who do nothing because they are too high to realize what is happening, or even undercover officers in the house to make a buy. Every cop has to exercise extreme control and do their job exactly as they are trained or it becomes total disaster. Like this case in Houston:

> houston police shoot man in back 9 times in botched drug raid, killing him; no drugs found.
> On July 12, 1998, members of a Houston Police anti-gang task force shot Pedro Oregon Navarro 12 times, killing him, during a warrantless drug raid on his apartment. A mistaken belief that a fellow officer had been shot during the raid supposedly prompted the barrage of gunfire, according to a Houston Police Department spokesperson. Officer Lamont E. Tillery, 30, was shot during the raid, but ballistics tests revealed that he had been shot by a fellow officer. (*Houston Chronicle*, July 13, 1998)

Fortunately this is not a typical incident. When everything goes right, meaning nobody gets hurt and the house is secured, the cops can settle down to the job of searching people and the house for weapons and drugs. Once everyone is secured, the narcotics officers come in to do their thing with the suspects. This is where we sometimes have problems. Everyone in the house is face down on the floor in handcuffs. With their hands behind their back, the cuffs are painful, even when properly applied. If there are a large number of suspects, the cops drape towels or other items over their heads to keep them from talking to each other.

As cops step over the suspects, their boots may "accidentally" come in contact" with those who can't identify them. Or they may threaten to hurt them if they don't tell where the drugs or guns are hidden. It's a game to the cops. Besides, they're just drug dealers and most cops don't care what happens to drug dealers. In fact, if it were up to most cops, drug dealers would only be arrested once and then they would be locked up forever. We see, up close and personal, on a daily basis, the devastating effects of illegal drug use. We know the damage crack cocaine, heroin, and meth-amphetamines are causing. It's gut wrenching to watch. So if all it takes is a little use of the Code to lock up the cause of the devasta-tion, then why not? Except that drug selling is not the problem, drug addiction is.

WHAT COULD POSSIBLY GO WRONG

Over the years, I experienced occasional problems with a particular team of narcotics officers. They were good investigators, but they had a tendency to use their fists instead of their mouths to question handcuffed prisoners. After one particular warrant, I told them I would personally walk them into the FBI office if I ever saw it hap-pen again. They got the message and things had gone pretty well for a while. A few months later, that same team had a warrant for a noto-rious crack dealer. Multiple agencies had been working on this guy for years, and now it was my team's rotation on warrant service.

We planned to use a front-end loader and take out the whole front corner of the house with the huge bucket, then rush in to take the heavily armed and barricaded dealers. I'd done over 300 high-risk warrants by this time, and I had a hand-picked team of some of the best officers in the unit. There was a lot of planning and organizing, but at the last minute, just hours before we were scheduled to execute, the narcotics team called it off. They had gone to the house, and it was empty. The doors were standing open, and no one was around. We had waited a day too long. They had found out we were coming.

About an hour later, I got a call from the same narcotics team. They were really unhappy about the events of the night, but they still wanted to do a simple warrant on a crack house that just opened up. They were sure there were no barricades. It would be a quick knock-down-the-front-door-with-the-ram and secure the two dealers inside. It sounded easy enough. What could go wrong?

I did the reconnaissance, put together a plan on how we would approach, what types of weapons we would carry, equipment to bring, etc. We hit the house three hours later. We went directly to the front door and swung the ram directly on the lockset. The lock shattered, the door started to open and then SLAM it was shut again. We hit it again with the ram. This time we watched it push against a scissors gate that was bolted to the inside walls on both sides of the door. Slam, it was shut again. In a very risky move, two officers pushed on the door while the officer with the lock buster shotgun took one shot at a key point on the gate. It flew open and we were in.

Inside were two runaway teens from Chicago. It didn't take long to find out they had been put to work by the very guy we were trying to get on the earlier warrant. These were not seasoned drug dealers. They were scared kids. They talked voluntarily to the narcotics officers, so we moved the whole team inside the house and out of sight. Part of the narcotics team interviewed the kids in one room while the other half of the team continued to arrest the crack cocaine buyers who kept lining up at the back window of the house.

After an hour or so someone knocked at the front door. I happened to be standing just inside the door, so I opened it to see a man dressed in a running jacket and pants and tennis shoes. He stepped in, looked at me, hesitated for a split second and then, as I reached for him, he bolted back out the door. It must have been the uniform, police hat, submachine gun, level three body armor and gun belt that scared him off. He took off running down the steps and across the street. I chased him between the houses and saw him start into an open garage, come out right away, and then run down the alley. I lost sight of him in the alley but as I ran out of gas, a much younger and very fit officer, who was behind me the whole way, kept up the chase. Within minutes he was walking our visitor back, undamaged, in handcuffs.

When we got back to the house, the senior narcotics officers recognized him. They questioned him in a back room. When they came out they asked me if I had seen him throw the dope he was supposed to be delivering? I told them I had not. They were very disappointed. They were sure it couldn't be too far away. A group of us, including some narcotics officers, retraced the path of the foot chase. On the garage floor, where the suspect had entered, was a softball-size clear plastic baggie of packaged-for-sale crack cocaine. Now the narcotics officers were ecstatic.

When we got back to the dope house with the evidence, the narcotics supervisor said he would meet me in transcription to dictate my report of the foot chase. He wanted to make sure I detailed how I saw the man I was chasing throw the baggie of crack cocaine into the garage. I told him I would be happy to meet him in transcription and report that I had seen the man run in and out of the garage. I could not and would not say I saw him throw anything. I never saw anything in his hands because it was dark, and the suspect had his back to me the entire time.

The narcotics supervisor looked confused and furious. I'm sure he assumed that, since this was a narcotics deal, we would all abide by the Code. It probably never occurred to him I would do otherwise. He brought over several other narcotics officers from his team, and they formed a very close circle around me. They bombarded me with accusations about my loyalty, my abilities, and my lack of understanding on how things were going to work. I told them I had no doubt the suspect had thrown the baggie of crack cocaine into the garage when he ducked inside, but I was not going to lie about it.

The supervisor finally gave up and told me I didn't have to do any paperwork if I was going to be like that. He would do the reports and say I saw the suspect throw the baggie. I told him that was his prerogative, but when it got to federal court, which I was sure it would, I would call him a liar on the stand if I was called to testify. He left very angry, and that team never asked me to help them with another warrant.

As it turned out, they didn't need me to lie. They found the suspects fingerprints all over the baggie and the whole team of narcotics cops were heroes. I think they even received some well deserved awards for their work that night. This time they were forced to do it right, but it didn't have to be that way. They could have done it the right way from the beginning. But, when "convict and incarcerate" becomes more important than "protect and serve," that is the kind of behavior the community gets from its cops.

Look at what former police chief Joseph D. McNamara has to say:

> Not many people took defense attorney Alan M. Dershowitz seriously when he charged that Los Angeles cops are taught to lie at the birth of their careers at the Police Academy. But as someone who spent 35 years wearing a police uniform, I've come to believe that hundreds of thousands of law-enforcement officers commit felony perjury every year testifying about drug arrests. These are not cops who take bribes or commit other crimes. Other than routinely lying, we are law-abiding and dedicated. We don't feel lying under oath is wrong because politicians tell them we are engaged in a "holy war" fighting evil. Then, too, the "enemy" these mostly white cops are testifying against are poor blacks and Latinos. (Joseph D. McNamara, "Has the Drug War Created an Officer Liars' Club?" *Los Angeles Times*, February 11, 1996)

You could argue that lying about this drug dealer was expedient and justified given the circumstances. After all, we would be taking a major threat to public safety out of circulation, and I knew he threw that baggie of crack into the garage, even if I didn't see it. But when we allow cops to operate on what they "know" as opposed to the evidence at hand we are asking for trouble.

Let me give you two examples. In the 1980s there were three rapes of women using the bus line that ran one block from my home. A suspect had been arrested, and investigators were working hard to get him charged. I happened to be in the courthouse in plain clothes when one of the investigators asked if I would be willing to stand in on a line up. I was generally the same size, age and race as the suspect. I agreed to help.

One woman picked me out immediately as the suspect. She told investigators she remembered me and recognized my face (although in her statement she already told the detectives she never saw her assailant's face). The other two women picked out the real rapist, and he was later convicted. When the investigator told the woman who picked me out that I lived in the neighborhood she realized she knew me from activities at the school our children attended.

Now here is where things could have gone wrong. During the times the women were raped, I was on my way home from work. I drove in the area of the rapes at the time they were occurring. I had no alibi and no witnesses to prove otherwise. DNA was not yet automatically accepted as evidence and my physical appearance was similar to the rapists. I could have ended up like Steve Avery:

> On July 29, 1985, a woman was brutally attacked, sexually assaulted, and nearly killed on a beach in Manitowoc County, Wisconsin. Steven Avery was charged with and

convicted of the brutal attack, based almost entirely on
eyewitness identification testimony of a single witness.
[A] DNA test conclusively excluded Avery as the source
of the pubic hair, and also identified the true perpetra-
tor of this crime, a man named Gregory Allen, who is
currently serving a 60-year sentence in prison for sexual
assaults committed after this one. September 11, 2003,
Avery walked out of the Stanley Correctional Institution.
He had served over 18 years in prison for a crime he did
not commit. (Truth in Justice.org/avery.htm)

What if the woman that picked me out had been the only victim?
What if these cops were more interested in getting a conviction
than getting at the truth? What if the investigator was the same cop
that threatened to kill me a few years earlier? See the problem? I
don't know that the cops or prosecutors did anything illegal in the
Steven Avery case. Let's assume that they were just very aggressive
crime fighters pursuing justice after a truly horrific crime. What
would they be willing to do to make sure they got a conviction?
Especially if they had the community pushing them to get this dangerous psychopath out of "their" neighborhood.

The *Journal Sentinel* also reported Sunday that its review
of more than 1,000 pages of court documents and law
enforcement reports suggests that authorities made Avery
a suspect so quickly that the case became a virtual steam-
roller. (*Milwaukee Herald Times*, September 2003)

What would a cop be willing to do behind the Code to secure a conviction, and some notoriety, for a conviction in this case?

> The assault victim told the Journal Sentinel that photos of Avery and the other prisoner show they looked so much alike that they could have been brothers, but authorities at the time showed her only a photo of Avery—even though the other man had been caught two years earlier for exposing himself and trying to grab a woman in the same area. (*Milwaukee Herald Times*, September 2003)

This wasn't an investigation conducted by one cop. There had to be many officers involved in the interviewing of witnesses.

> Sixteen witnesses, including Avery's family and friends, a cement contractor, and clerks at Shopko, along with store receipts from Shopko, corroborated Avery's alibi. But the state didn't believe Avery or his 16 alibi witnesses. (Truth in Justice.org/avery.htm)

Maybe the "state" didn't believe Avery, but I am willing to bet there was at least one cop who did. Where was that cop when witnesses were testifying on Avery's behalf? Where were the cops, and let's not forget the prosecutors, who knew what investigators had done in the photo lineup? The Code would have kept them from talking to anyone but each other. Even cops who believed Avery was innocent would have kept their mouths shut. They probably never considered making an argument for Avery's innocence. The Code doesn't allow us to question other cops, especially when the community gets behind the cops who are perverting the system. The community wants to feel safe, and they expect the cops to protect them. But what did they do to themselves in the Avery case? They let the real rapist run free in their midst, committing more sexual assaults, while they focused on making sure "someone paid" for this heinous crime. My story could have been Steven Avery's story.

About the time my first edition of *Walking With The Devil* was going to print Avery was arrested again. Here was a man just waiting to be convicted of his next violent crime. His criminal history included burglary, animal cruelty, assault, sex crimes, and weapons crimes.

The following is from an Associated Press article.

TIMELINE IN THE STEVEN AVERY MURDER CASE

2005

Oct. 31—Teresa Halbach, 25, of St. John in Calumet County, a photographer for Auto Trader Magazine goes to Avery's Auto Salvage near Mishicot, a rural area in Manitowoc County 90 miles north of Milwaukee.

The salvage yard is run by the family of Steven Avery, 44, who was freed from prison in 2003 after DNA evidence cleared him of a 1985 rape for which he served 18 years. Avery has said Halbach took pictures of a minivan he had for sale and left.

Nov. 3—Halbach's family reports her missing, and authorities launch an investigation.

Nov. 5—Volunteer searchers find Halbach's vehicle under brush and auto parts in the Avery salvage yard.

Nov. 8—Avery tells reporters he fears authorities are trying to frame him because he sued Manitowoc County officials for $36 million for his wrongful conviction.

Nov. 9—Avery is arrested and, based past convictions for burglary and other crimes, charged with possessing firearms as a felon. Authorities say they found two guns in his trailer home.

Nov. 15—Steven Avery is charged with first-degree intentional homicide and mutilating a corpse. He is ordered held on $500,000 bail.

2006

Feb. 14—Authorities announce Avery has settled his lawsuit against Manitowoc County officials for $400,000.

Feb. 15—The Halbach family files a wrongful death suit against Avery.

March 2—Avery's nephew Brendan Dassey, then 16, is charged in adult court with being a party to first-degree intentional homicide, mutilation of a corpse and first-degree sexual assault. A criminal complaint quotes Dassey as saying that when he went to Avery's trailer after school on Oct. 31, he heard a woman call "Help me." He says he found Halbach shackled on Avery's bed and the two raped and killed her.

March 24—The Halbachs add Dassey to their wrongful death suit.

March 31—Avery tells The Associated Press that he thinks investigators coerced Dassey into a confession because Dassey is not very smart.

Aug. 22—A judge moves Avery's trial from Manitowoc County to Calumet County but says jurors will be chosen in Manitowoc County.

Sept. 1—A judge schedules Dassey's trial for April 16 in Manitowoc County.

Sept. 25—A judge says Avery's past crimes cannot be used as evidence when he goes on trial. Court records and police say Avery's criminal history includes burglary, animal abuse and the attempted abduction of a Mishicot woman in 1984.

2007

Jan. 29—A judge dismisses sexual assault and kidnapping charges against Avery because of the uncertainty of Dassey's testimony.

Jan. 30—A judge allows as evidence an unsecured sample of Avery's blood, which his attorneys say supports their claim that he was framed. The judge also says defense attorneys can tell jurors that Avery was wrongly convicted of rape.

Feb. 9—Attorneys picked eight women and eight men from Manitowoc County to serve as Avery's jury.

Feb. 12—The trial begins with attorneys giving their opening statements.

March 12—After the prosecution and defense rest, the judge dismisses a false-imprisonment charge, saying he didn't think the jury had enough evidence to find Avery guilty. He refuses to dismiss the remaining charges of murder, mutilating a corpse and being a felon in possession of a firearm.

March 15—Following closing arguments by both sides, the jury deliberates about 4½ hours before retiring for the night.

March 16—The judge dismisses a male juror because of a family emergency and replaces him with a female alternate, who had also been sequestered. The judge orders the jury to start deliberations anew.

March 18—After deliberating for nearly 22 hours over three days, jurors convict Avery of the charges of first-degree intentional homicide and being a felon in possession of a firearm. Avery is acquitted of the charge of mutilating a corpse.

Manitowoc County Circuit Judge Patrick Willis reviewed Avery's history of convictions for burglaries, threatening a woman with a gun and dousing a cat with gasoline before throwing it in a bonfire, before sentencing him. The offenses escalated over time, Willis said, and the latest one—Halbach's murder—was a "calculated" case of premeditated murder.

"You are probably the most dangerous individual ever
to set foot in this courtroom," [Judge] Willis said Friday.
"From what I see nothing in your life suggests that society would ever be safe from your behavior."[6]

As a cop my gut tells me that Avery should have been locked
up forever, long before he was found guilty of the rape he didn't
commit. Was it a mistake to release him? No, because as long as
everyone believed that Avery was the rapist, the real rapist was
free to rape again, and he did. Did it have a disastrous ending? Yes.
That is the nature of evil, and if you stay in this job long enough
you will have your own list of people that should never see day-
light again. This is the ancient battle of good versus evil and we
must always remember that we are the good and the code of silence
can only bring us to the side of evil.

How strong is the temptation, based on our emotions, to walk
with the devil and put people like Steven Avery in prison forever?
It's overwhelming. Every time we read a story like this it fuels the
fires of our passion to do *whatever it takes*, regardless of the evidence,
to protect the Teresa Halbachs of the world. But the truth is, there
will be more Teresa Halbachs. Every generation of cops has seen, and
will see, the senseless and cruel death of innocents. We know that as
peace officers we owe it to the community and each other to ensure
that we do what we can, within the law, to prevent those deaths. But
we must not forget that we owe it to our fellow officers to also protect them from themselves so they do not sacrifice themselves and
their families for the sake of a battle, and lose everything in return.

Here's another example, albeit on a much lighter note. My younger brother was riding in the squad with me on a very busy hot summer night. We received a call to a robbery/assault that just occurred a block away. When we got there, the medics were already loading the victim into the ambulance. I had only a minute to get a quick statement from the badly-beaten victim. As I was getting the information, my brother stepped closer to hear. The victim looked up at him and with a terrified look in his eyes, pointed to my brother and said, "THAT'S HIM!! THAT'S THE GUY WHO ROBBED ME!"

It is not unusual for a psychotic or acquaintance robber to check on his victim, and the officers standing behind my brother immediately grabbed him. The poor guy. I've never seen his eyes get so big. I told the other cops who he was, and they let him go, laughing about his reaction to being accused. My point is that if you have less than ethical police investigators and prosecutors, there can be grave injustices.

What do you think happened in these cases?

> Texas—Rape victim identifies assailant on the street. After four years in prison DNA excludes him and he is set free.
>
> Rhode Island—Police officer convicted of murdering his wife. Six years in prison due to an incompetent coroner who botched the autopsy. Exonerated and reinstated to police department.
>
> Illinois—Son wrongfully sentenced to death for the murder of his parents. The true murderer is discovered several years later after his case was reversed and remanded.

Maryland—The first capital conviction in the United States overturned as a result of DNA testing. After serving almost ten years in prison, including two on death row, another man was charged with the murder for which he was wrongfully convicted.

Illinois—Son is wrongly charged in July 2000 with the murder of his mother after he gave a video taped confession, which Chicago police detectives elicited after more than 50 hours of interrogation. Exonerated after almost a year and a half in custody when DNA evidence proved another man had committed the crime.
(The Justice Project)

Most people don't believe you can be convicted by a jury of a crime you didn't commit—but you can—when "convict and incarcerate" becomes more important than "protect and serve." What do you think the cops from these previous cases do when the issue is drunk driving or speeding? Do you trust them to "know" what is right? Are you willing to let them decide when to lie "in the pursuit of justice?" Now tell me you think it's all right for cops to lie, as long as they "know" what happened.

CREATIVE REPORT WRITING—MASTERS LEVEL

Ironically, unethical cops with great writing and/or technical skills are often very successful. Their cases get prosecuted because the probable cause is always perfect and the evidence is always seized at exactly the right time. These officers can become the shining stars of their departments. I will give you two real examples.

Officer number one was in charge of a very high-profile unit. He and his officers made lots and lots of felony arrests of mostly black men because they set up their operations in mostly black neighborhoods. (Please tell me you can see the problem here.) They received numerous complaints and were constantly in the paper for alleged abuses of force, racist or derogatory language, and racial profiling.

I was working in Internal Affairs at the time, and in one of several complaints brought against this unit, a friend of mine, a black man, came in to make a complaint. My friend called for police assistance on a prowler. When the officers arrived, one of them shoved a handgun into his mouth that left abrasions on the roof of his mouth. I recommended a finding of "sustained" for excessive force, but the chief liked the fact that this unit was targeting criminals. He gave the complaint a "not sustained." In other words, the chief did not agree the lacerations were proof of the alleged complaint—maybe he thought it was a bad toothbrush! Not long afterward, this same team of officers accidentally shot a man to death after jamming a shotgun into his forehead.

> September 21, 1984, Minneapolis, Minnesota.
> Sal Saran Scott: Shot in the face at point-blank range after being arrested by a Minneapolis police officer who was a member of the controversial decoy unit. The shooting was considered accidental . . . (Communities United Against Police Brutality)

There is no way to know for sure, but I still believe that if the chief had held this group of officers accountable and not let them hide behind the Code, that fatal shooting might never have occurred.

This unit was arresting a lot of people, and their reports were always a model of report writing perfection. But they got careless with their lies, and a presumably straightforward case was found "not guilty" by a jury. At the end of the trial, a court officer noticed that photocopies of evidence supposedly taken hours apart by separate officers (the officers testified to this) were exact duplicates of the same money—a single photocopy, duplicated, and submitted as separate pieces of evidence.

The two officers put their own initials, date, and time on each of two identical copies and submitted them to the court as evidence of the theft taken before and after the crime. Then they testified in court as to their veracity. It was pure and simple perjury by the cops. Now, it was not the sergeant in charge who testified or initialed the photocopies, but where do you suppose the officers learned their behavior? Can you believe for even one minute that it was the only time they lied?

> Minneapolis Police Chief Tony Bouza has decided to discipline ten former members of the decoy squad, capping a six-month investigation into allegations of tainted and mishandled evidence that has resulted in the dismissal of 27 criminal cases. (Kevin Diaz, *Minneapolis Star Tribune,* June 28, 1986)

This supervisor was later rewarded by being assigned to command the Internal Affairs Unit.

Another example. Officer number two is a modern-day hero. This officer has done some truly heroic deeds and like number one is very bright. Officer number two figured out the system very quickly: 1) no one likes drug dealers; 2) drug dealers lie when they deny wrongdoing; 3) the administration and the citizens love it when drug dealers are dealt with; and 4) most importantly, the paperwork has to be perfect if any drug dealer is going to get charged.

Officer number two has more successful street drug prosecutions than anyone in the precinct. In fact, within the precinct, any "perfect" drug arrest reports and follow-up warrants are tagged with the officer's nickname if there is any indication the probable cause was *adjusted* to meet the needs of the warrant. The other cops talk about it, but they don't tell the public what's going on because officer number two receives awards from community groups and the officer's own agency for the outstanding work, and drug dealers are going to prison. Like many other cops, he has also done some truly courageous, innovative, and legal police work.

There are citizens who would praise this officer for being creative, even if they knew the whole story. But cops and citizens who support an unethical cop today because that cop is arresting drug dealers need to remember that same cop will just as easily lie about them or their children in a traffic case, accident investigation, or excessive force investigation. Is that OK with you? It takes a lot of hard work to put together a good arrest on the street. Evidence at a

crime scene and probable cause for an arrest are almost never perfect. Even after a lot of hard work and long hours, a case will occasionally still fall apart, so the Code has great power here. It can *fix*
your problems. If that's all it takes, why should a cop be completely
honest and beat his head against the wall to make a legitimate case
when he or she sees all the glory going to officers who use good
writing skills in place of good probable cause?

Gary Sudduth, God rest his soul, was the executive director of
the Minneapolis Urban League when he told me that black teenag-
ers hate the cops. He did not have one single suggestion on how to
correct the problem given the current culture of policing. He went
on to say there are cops working in the minority community who
lie, use excessive force, and target people of color. Not all of them,
he conceded, but enough to taint every officer and, as a result, the
community has lost faith in the police department. This hate doesn't
just stem from seeing bad cops do bad acts. More than anything, it
grows out of the community's frustration with the good cops who
do nothing to stop it.

> The loyalty ethic and insularity that breed the code of
> silence that protects officers from other officers also erects
> protective barriers between the police and the public.
> (Mollen 1994, 58)

Here is one example of community damage in progress from a
Minnesota study on racial profiling.

A basic pattern emerges from our analysis of traffic stop data collected by the sixty-five law enforcement jurisdictions that voluntarily participated in this racial profiling study:

Law enforcement officers stopped Black, Latino, and American Indian drivers at greater rates than White drivers, searched Blacks, Latinos, and American Indians at greater rates than White drivers, and found contraband as a result of searches of Blacks, Latinos, and American Indians at lower rates than in searches of White drivers. Conversely, law enforcement officers stopped and searched White drivers at lower rates than drivers of color and found contraband in searches of White drivers at a greater rate than in searches of drivers of color.

These disparities are particularly large for Blacks and Latinos. . . .

The pattern for Blacks and Latinos existed in nearly every participating jurisdiction. . . .

These disparities in discretionary search rates are particularly troubling given the rates at which contraband was found as a result of these searches, i.e. the hit rates. Overall, 24% of discretionary searches of Whites produced contraband compared to only 11% of searched of Blacks and 9% of searches of Latinos. In the 37 jurisdictions where discretionary searches of both Blacks and Whites occurred, the hit rate was higher for Whites in 30 of the jurisdictions. In 31 of the 44 jurisdictions where there were discretionary searches of both Whites and Latinos the hit rate was higher for Whites.

The greatest relative differences between actual and expected stops and searches for Blacks are found in suburban cities and central cities other than Minneapolis. In the suburban cities of Fridley, New Hope, Plymouth, Sauk Rapids, and Savage combined, Blacks were stopped about 310% more often than expected. Once stopped, officers subjected Blacks to discretionary searches at a rate 108% greater than expected even though only 11% of Blacks were found in possession of contraband compared to 18% of Whites searched. . . .

The largest absolute differences between actual and expected stops and searches for Blacks and Latinos were found in Minneapolis, the largest jurisdiction participating in this study with the highest number of traffic stops. In Minneapolis, Blacks were stopped 152% more often than expected and once stopped, subjected to discretionary searches 52% more often than expected. . . .

The greatest relative differences between actual and expected stops and searches for Blacks are found in suburban cities and central cities other than Minneapolis. In the suburban cities of Fridley, New Hope, Plymouth, Sauk Rapids, and Savage combined, Blacks were stopped about 310% more often than expected. Once stopped, officers subjected Blacks to discretionary searches at a rate 108% greater than expected even though only 11% of Blacks were found in possession of contraband compared to 18% of Whites searched. . . .

The largest absolute differences between actual and expected stops and searches for Blacks and Latinos were found in Minneapolis, the largest jurisdiction participat-

ing in this study with the highest number of traffic stops.
In Minneapolis, Blacks were stopped 152% more often
than expected and once stopped, subjected to discretionary searches 52% more often than expected. . . .

These patterns suggest a strong likelihood that racial/
ethnic bias plays a role in traffic stop policies and practices in Minnesota. The same is true for the searches that
result from these stops. Taken together, these patterns
warrant serious examination. It is fair to conclude that the
problems that they suggest are not isolated to a handful
of jurisdictions or present only in those jurisdictions that
chose to participate in this study. . . ."[7]

One of our more affluent St. Paul suburbs was known for stopping any male who wasn't white. A black officer I knew told me
he was stopped every time he drove through there in his own car.
Once, when he identified himself as a cop, the young cop who
stopped him had the balls to tell him they stop every black male
who drives through their community—"It's department policy." As
if my friend, since he was a cop, would understand. When they got
a new chief, the policy changed. Now explain to me, "Why exactly
should the minority community trust us?" They know some of
us lie and the rest of us tolerate it. Even if they believe only a few
cops lie, they know the good cops don't do anything to correct the
problem. In other words, the good cops are refusing to protect the
community they serve from the bad cops. On that basis alone, why
should the minority community believe we are being truthful when
we talk about more important issues like police shootings or alleged
sexual assaults?

We are known by our actions, not by our words, and we have allowed the Code of Silence to dictate those less-than-honorable actions.

OUR RECENT HISTORY—IT'S NOT PRETTY

New knowledge is interpreted in the context of existing knowledge. As new cops, we view the world in the context of our own upbringing and education, and we assume, usually wrongly, that other people see the world the same way we do. We have attended all the required classes in minority relations, diversity, and crisis communications, and we hit the street ready to be a model of tolerance and compassion. But we get frustrated and angry when confronted by men and women who are also frustrated and angry with the way they have been treated in the past.

A lot of young cops don't realize there are many in the community who remember a time when minority relations meant being beaten by cops while other cops watched, or being unable to enter a store with a "whites only" sign on the door. A good number of these men and women are now in their 50s and 60s and have taken leadership roles in our communities. Many are good people who may have forgiven, but have not forgotten, the injustices of the past. They know what cops are capable of when they hide behind the Code.

The Vera Institute of Justice takes us back to February 6, 1968, when students from South Carolina State College in Orangeburg protested the refusal of Harry Floyd to desegregate his bowling alley. At a bonfire rally that night, cops and FBI agents were present when a student threw a fence post at one of the cops. The cops responded by shooting thirty students, killing three.

When the state and the local prosecutors made no effort to prosecute the cops responsible, the federal civil rights division stepped in. Local police officials instructed officers not to cooperate with federal investigators, including those from the FBI. Following eight days of testimony, the federal grand jury refused to indict. The Federal Civil Rights Division decided to bring the patrolmen to trial by filing a criminal information. It alleged that eight patrolmen willfully fired at students "with the intent of imposing summary punishment upon those persons," thereby violating their constitutional right "not to be deprived of life or liberty without due process of law." But it was for naught. The trial jury came back "not guilty" for all eight cops.

This is not ancient history. The "Orangeburg Massacre" occurred while my dad was still a cop and I was about to enter the U.S. Air Force. And it was not an isolated incident. People may forgive, but they don't forget. Like I said at the beginning of this section, new knowledge is interpreted in the context of existing knowledge. The minority community understands the history of racism in policing better than we do. Right or wrong, their interpretation of the police use of force will be a lot different than ours. It would be easy to say most police misconduct is racist since so many high-profile cases of police malfeasance involve minorities, but I don't believe that's true. Take the following two stories.

In her book *A Rip in Heaven* (2004), Jeanine Cummins tells the gruesome story of a 1991 murder in St. Louis. A white male is accused by the police of murdering his cousins after he "confessed" following twelve hours of interrogation and a failed lie detector test. The actual murdering rapists were four black men from St. Louis, one of whom confesses and tells investigators the whole story. Three were given the death sentence, and one was given thirty years.

Now let's take an even more current example from this Associated Press report in the *Minneapolis Star Tribune,* June 11, 2004.

> new york—Martha Stewart asked a judge Thursday to grant her a new trial, citing charges that a government witness at her first trial lied repeatedly on the stand. . . . The motion argues that the conviction is tainted by newly unveiled perjury charges against Larry Stewart, a Secret Service laboratory director who was called as an expert witness at the trial in February. . . . The filing said several other Secret Service officials were in court, monitoring the trial, and were aware of the alleged perjury but did not speak up. "Their silence is scandalous and not the way we expect the government to conduct itself," Martha Stewart's lawyers, Robert Morvillo and John Tigue, said in a statement.

What is the community supposed to think about the Secret Service based on these actions?

Cops who lie will lie about anyone. Race is not the issue. Integrity is!

THE RIPPLE EFFECT

Just one officer hitting a suspect in handcuffs or lying about drug arrests creates a "ripple effect" in the community that reaches everyone. When another officer stands there and tolerates that kind of abuse, there is a tremendous loss of respect for all cops. Soon, everyone "knows" the cops use excessive force and that we hit people in handcuffs. So, just like the cop "knows" the drug dealer had the drugs in his hand, the community "knows" all cops are brutal. We have taught the community how to define the word "know" by the way we "know" what the truth is. Worst of all, when things go badly after a police shooting or other critical incident, all those "small lies" catch up with us, and it is often the honest cop or innocent citizen who suffers.

When cops begin to operate on the basis of what we "know" as opposed to what the evidence proves, there will always be grave injustices. We've all seen it. Look at the history of the Los Angeles Police Department and compare what was going on in the Rampart Division—murder, planting guns, planting evidence, and stealing cocaine from the property room—with the response to Rodney King. You have to believe the community was aware of how these rotten cops were acting. It was only a few of them, *but other cops did nothing to stop them!*

According to the Innocence Project there have been **265 post-conviction DNA exonerations** in the United States.

- The first DNA exoneration took place in 1989. Exonerations have been won in **34 states**; since 2000, there have been 198 exonerations.
- 17 of the 265 people exonerated through DNA **served time on death row.**
- The average length of time served by exonerees is 13 years. The total number of years served is approximately 3,433.
- The average age of exonerees at the time of their wrongful convictions was 27.

Races of the 265 exonerees:
158 African Americans, 80 Caucasians, 21 Latinos, 2 Asian Americans, 4 whose race is unknown. The true suspects and/or perpetrators have been identified in **116 of the DNA exoneration cases.**

- Since 1989, there have been tens of thousands of cases where prime suspects were identified and pursued—until DNA testing (prior to conviction) proved that they were wrongly accused.
- In more than 25 percent of cases in a National Institute of Justice study, suspects were excluded once DNA testing was conducted during the criminal investigation (the study, conducted in 1995, included 10,060 cases where testing was performed by FBI labs).
- About half of the people exonerated through DNA testing have been financially compensated. 27 states, the federal government, and the District of Columbia have

passed laws to compensate people who were wrongfully incarcerated. Awards under these statutes vary from state to state.

• 22 percent of cases closed by the Innocence Project since 2004 were closed because of lost or missing evidence.

Leads such as hair microscopy, bite mark comparisons, firearm tool mark analysis and shoe print comparisons—have never been subjected to rigorous scientific evaluation. Meanwhile, forensics techniques that have been properly validated—such as serology, commonly known as blood typing—are sometimes improperly conducted or inaccurately conveyed in trial testimony. In other wrongful conviction cases, forensic scientists have engaged in misconduct.

False confessions and incriminating statements lead to wrongful convictions in approximately 25 percent of cases. In 35 percent of false confession or admission cases, the defendant was 18 years old or younger and/or developmentally disabled. Twenty-two of the first 265 DNA exonerees **pled guilty** to crimes they did not commit. The Innocence Project encourages police departments to electronically record all custodial interrogations in their entirety in order to prevent coercion and to provide an accurate record of the proceedings. More than 500 jurisdictions have voluntarily adopted policies to record interrogations. State supreme courts have taken action in Alaska, Massachusetts, Minnesota, New Hampshire, New Jersey, and Wisconsin. Illinois, Maine, New Mexico, and the District of Columbia require the taping of interrogations in homicide cases."[8]

Yet cops continue to push the limits of the constitution in order to get convictions. Take the case of Joyce Gilchrist. The following is from a *Washington Post* editorial dated May 28, 2001:

> For the latest exhibit of the fallibility of the judicial system, we turn to Joyce Gilchrist, a chemist with the Oklahoma City Police Department who has worked on more than 3,000 cases. Oklahoma has executed 11 persons based at least in part on her work. Twelve more remain on death row.
>
> Yet in recent weeks the FBI labs have been sharply critical of her performance in a sample of cases, accusing her of offering testimony "beyond the acceptable limits of forensic science" in several. Jeffrey Pierce recently was released from prison for a rape he didn't commit; Ms. Gilchrist's testimony at his trial had authoritatively linked his hair to samples found at the scene, a claim DNA testing later belied. A comprehensive review of Ms. Gilchrist's work is now underway. The alleged problems with Ms. Gilchrist's work are not new. According to the *Daily Oklahoman*, a professional association criticized her as far back as 1987. State and federal courts have overturned convictions on grounds that her testimony went beyond what was knowable scientifically. Last year she was expelled from another professional group. Ms. Gilchrist says she will be vindicated by the investigation.
>
> But questions about her work serve as a reminder of the grave harm that a single person in the criminal justice apparatus can cause—either through malice or incompetence—if the rest of the system offers little more than malign neglect.

For an unethical cop, it is often easier to make the evidence fit the suspect than to let the evidence speak for itself. Amazingly, there are seldom any negative consequences for the officers involved in these cases. But a word of warning: police agencies that protect cops to avoid civil penalties penalize all of us because cops who lie about crooks will lie about anyone. Equally important, a community that tolerates lies and abuse by its cops in the name of the "war on drugs and crime" risks subjecting every citizen to the same fate as those it prosecutes.

COLLABORATIVE POWER

Let me give you another firsthand example of how we use our collaborative power to protect our cop culture. It's not exactly a Code of Silence issue, but I think you will see how it fits in with the Code mindset. In 1995, I designed a research experiment as part of an academic assignment. I used the high failure rate of Asian officer candidates in the Minneapolis Police Field Training Program as a starting point.

The Minneapolis Police Department actively recruits people of color, though they have not had great success. And even though the official policy is to have a police department that is representative of its citizenry, only 17 percent of the department claimed minority status in 2003 compared with a city-wide population made up of 35 percent minorities.

Two Asian males were recruited and trained. Both passed recruit school but failed in the Field Training Program. The majority

of the Field Training Officers who gave failing marks to these officers were white males, but racial and ethnic biases were denied by
the officers. One of the failed officers was given a second chance at
the academy (with my full support). Near the end of the academy
we carefully choreographed a series of incidents involving the use
of force by a lone uniformed officer. The officer's actions were carefully scripted to be exactly what we would expect from a graduating recruit. I videotaped the actions from directly overhead, using
the fully uniformed Asian officer who was about to graduate from
the academy and start his Field Training Program a second time.
His face was not visible under his police hat.

I showed the video tape at a south-side precinct and told them
I wanted their opinions on the use of force tactics in the video. The
majority approved of the officer's actions. I took the video to the
precinct where the Asian officer would be assigned for his FTO
training and made a point of identifying the Asian officer in the
video prior to viewing. This group of officers *failed* him on most of
his actions—actions that were just what we would expect from a
graduating rookie.

I showed the report and the video to our department's legal
advisor. She was very unhappy. With much frustration in her voice
she told me, "Now we have to pass this candidate," as if that was
going to be a bad thing. This attorney was as smart and honest as
they come, but she never even mentioned the fact that we would
have lost this officer to bias. She was more concerned about setting a precedent within the training program. The bottom line is
the Asian officer passed the Field Training Program. The last time I

checked he was doing a good job as a street cop in spite of what the training officers had planned for him.

The police culture and the control of that culture through the Code of Silence are shaping the future of law enforcement. Everyone involved in the process of selection, recruitment, and training needs to be aware of the forces involved and look for ways to change that part of the culture.

TEACHING ETHICS TO COPS—OR NOT

I had the opportunity and displeasure to lead the first "ethics" class for in-service training in fifteen years in Minneapolis. I can't imagine why I volunteered for the job. Some of the most senior officers and supervisors on the department were in the first class, including many of the thieves and thugs I have been talking about. But, all in all, it didn't go as badly as it could have. Most of the cops realized I was covering mandated subjects, and they quietly suffered through it and avoided participating. So it was pretty boring stuff until I brought up a tactic Chicago crack dealers were using to corrupt street and narcotics officers. An angry shift commander immediately stood up and berated me for even insinuating that one of his officers could be corrupted by money. Taking no pity on him, I congratulated him on what must be his great leadership skills. Then I quickly reminded him it was an officer from his shift who was recently sent to prison for demanding sex from female traffic offenders.

He was quiet for the rest of the hour.

> Officer Michael Ray Parent: In the early morning hours of
> August 5, 1994, a woman motorist was stopped by Officer
> Parent, who asked her whether she had been drinking.
> She acknowledged she had been drinking, and he put
> her in the back seat of his squad car and told her she was
> under arrest for driving under the influence. He report-
> edly forced her to have oral sex with him, and he told her
> this was better than going to jail and having some woman
> have her way with her. (Human Rights Watch)

I probably could have been more tactful, but it was a great
example of how quickly we cover for police corruption within our
own ranks by just denying it. The sad thing is he wasn't trying to
cover for anyone. He is a good honest man, the kind of cop you
want in your community.

THE CODE AT THE EXECUTIVE LEVEL

I was in a high-level meeting with a large law enforcement agency.
We were discussing the importance of background checks. There
was one candidate I thought deserved a chance, but I was over-
ruled by the chief of the agency. Her comment to me was that she
had the final say on all applicants because it was important to find
people who would fit the mold of her organization. According to
her, this was one of the ways her agency avoided the problems

common to the Minneapolis Police Department. I guess she didn't count her two officers who went to trial for rape, or the officer from her department who was caught buying crack cocaine—in Minneapolis. I don't believe for even one minute she was trying to cover for anyone. But even in a room of only cops, she abided by the Code.

This is the insidious nature of the Code. It creates its own set of plausible myths. It seduces you to meld what you know with what you want to believe and, before long, the ends do begin to justify the means.

TRUSTING IN YOUR PARTNERS

By its very nature the choice to play or not to play the Code of Silence game is an individual choice, but we don't need to make these choices alone. We should be able to look to our partners for support in making good ethical decisions. Out of necessity, most cops learn to operate independently. It is this independent, discretionary nature of the job that can create mental barriers when it comes time to ask another cop for help on ethical issues. Let me show you what can happen when cops are willing to give up independence for interdependence.

In the Robbery/Decoy Unit, it was our job to target high-crime areas by presenting ourselves as victims, get robbed, and then arrest the perpetrators. We would use crime analysis to define the area we would work and identify the characteristics of the typical victim. On this particular night we were working in an area of downtown where there had been a number of particularly vicious assaults on drunks. The suspects would not only rob their victims, they would beat them up afterward.

We rotated the duty on our team, and it was my turn to play victim/drunk. I was standing in a little alcove when a man stood in front of me and started to ask me questions to determine how drunk I was. I knew there was another guy with him, but I had to keep my head down and play drunk so I could not see where he was in relation to me. I had on a fake Rolex watch that they fumbled with several times while asking me what time it was. I knew they were going for my drunken act and would eventually get the watch. I didn't anticipate how they were going to do it.

The guy in front of me lifted my head up to look directly at him. The second guy planted his feet, drew his arm back as far as he could reach, then hit me dead center in my right temple with a hard punch. I never saw it coming. One minute I was playing drunk and the next moment there was an enormous flash of bright light in my skull. Everything went into slow motion. In what seemed liked minutes of silent falling, I saw a series of gradually fading flashes that ended when I hit the ground on my hands and knees. I opened my eyes and saw a pair of feet preparing to kick me in the head. I responded with my gun in my hand lunging at the person coming toward me. I was in a rage. The first words I screamed at him were "FREEZE MOTHERFUCKER!!" Not exactly the "police—don't move" that I had been trained to use.

Kneeing him in the groin so hard he lifted off the ground, I drove him back into a recessed doorway, with my gun in my right hand and my left hand grabbing his shirt. But he grabbed me by the wrists and now we struggled for control of my gun. As the gun twisted back and forth, pointing at me then at him, I repeatedly threatened to "pull the fuckin' trigger."

But now the punch started to catch up with me. As my field of vision constricted to black, my body collapsed against his. I was falling into darkness again, and I couldn't stop it. I held on to the suspect as hard as I could. I heard a dull thump amid the mumbled voices in my head, and I strained to make sense of what was happening, but I had no control. When I came to again I was on my hands and knees; only this time the guy I was fighting with was underneath me.

My gun was cocked. Finger on the trigger it was pointed at his forehead from only inches away. When I collapsed, I squeezed with both hands and fired one round right alongside his head, tattooing his ear with gunpowder, and my gun had gone into single action. The bullet had missed his head by less than an inch as I fell on top of him. I still held onto his shirt.

As I got my senses back, he was reaching into his shirt to get something. I knew I was still in trouble and I threatened repeatedly to kill him if he didn't do exactly what I said. "I ought to just kill you right there Motherfucker. Get your hands out where I can see them!" Backup officers arrived; he went to jail, and I went for head and neck x-rays.

I share this event with you because the details of this assault came from the video we made from a surveillance van, not from my memory. When we watched and I heard the language I used and the threats I made to kill him, my first response was to erase the audio on the tape before anyone heard it. My language was a clear violation of at least three department rules, and I had just shot at a guy who had no weapon. I was in a panic over what would happen to me as a result of nearly killing this guy and the threats I had made. I would have done something stupid, like erasing the audio, if it had been left up to me at that moment.

Fortunately, I had a team of great cops working with me. They convinced me to submit the tape as it was. I had trusted these men and women with my life, now I trusted them with my career. It was the right thing to do. My reactions to that punch were not based on reason. They were based solely on survival but, being a reasoning man, it was incredibly hard for me to listen and believe anyone would approve of what I had done. But I trusted these cops. They were experienced, honest street cops. There was a terrible internal struggle between my gut and my brain, but I had to believe they were right no matter what my gut reaction was. So I won this battle with the Code, but only because my fellow officers did the right thing and supported me. I could not have done it alone. There is no way to predict what battles a cop will face or what he or she will do, but I do know that, with the support of other cops, the odds on winning are a lot better.

THE BEST JOB IN MY CAREER

I know that ethical policing works when cops support each other in right conduct. I supervised two units that refused to use the Code. In the Decoy Unit and Repeat Offender Program we targeted some of the most dangerous career criminals in the city. We never got a complaint of inappropriate language, excessive force, or racial profiling because we did the job the way it was supposed to be done. We were fair and honest, and when you work from that mindset there is seldom any need for the Code. Over fifteen years later, many of my former coworkers from both those units tell me it was the best job of their entire career, and they were tough jobs!

We often worked twenty-hour days and sometimes back-to-back shifts. Officers were expected to develop their own leads and informants; and we had no budget other than salaries. In our first year of operation, we drove cars that should have been condemned and used our own personal video cameras and other equipment. But even with all these limitations and the incredible expectation that we would arrest and imprison at least fifteen of the top forty career criminals, no one complained. The reason? There was no Code of Silence. It wasn't allowed. Were we tempted to use the Code? Sure. But we all supported a common ideal—fair and honest policing. If an officer in the unit felt something wasn't right, we talked about it and made it right. We held each other accountable for our actions.

It's not like we all loved each other. These were all smart, aggressive, hard-working cops with very strong personalities.

There were lots of highly-animated discussions on whose case had priority but, at the end of the day, it didn't matter whose case we worked on, because we all knew that once we started it was done the right way. It may seem counterintuitive, but this manner of operation eliminated the negative job stress you hear so many cops complain about because there was no BS, no hidden agenda, and no Code of Silence.

10 Myths of Policing

The great enemy of truth is very often not the lie—deliberate contrived and dishonest—but the myth—persistent, persuasive and realistic.

JOHN F. KENNEDY, YALE COMMENCEMENT, 1962

THE STREET WAY

A LOT OF THE POWER of the Code of Silence comes out of myths perpetuated by police trainers. Police training is typically done in two phases, academic training and field training. For the street cop there will always be two ways of doing everything—the "academy way" and the "street way," the street way often being defined by the Code.

The academic portion can take up to four years depending on what a department requires; but the field training is by far the most difficult. The Field Training Officer (FTO) takes a new cop with only academic training as her partner and responds to real calls with all the inherent dangers. She must assume the recruit will make mistakes and hopes the mistakes don't result in a loss of life, especially theirs. It is commonplace for the FTO to tell a recruit to "Forget everything you were taught at the academy. Just keep your mouth shut and your ears open." It may seem harsh, but the reasoning behind these comments comes from years of experience. In those first months of policing, the FTO is responsible for the recruit's survival. They know what they have done to survive, and they want their recruit to adopt those strategies for their own so they don't end up like this rookie.

> Officer Hamilton was shot and killed after being ambushed by a 14-year-old boy armed with an AR-15 rifle. The boy had just killed his father and called the police and ambushed Officer Hamilton and her partner when we arrived. The round that struck Officer Hamilton struck her in the armhole of her vest. The suspect committed suicide after firing upon the officers. Officer Hamilton had only been with the department for three months. She is survived by her father, brother, and two children. (Officer Down Memorial Page)

And though the academic training is rigorous, recruits still have a lot to learn before they can effectively apply their knowledge. Even with guided practice, a smart recruit will take months to function independently. It will be three to seven years before they are a seasoned vet. The trouble with most field training is the myths perpetuated through the years from cop to cop that are so destructive to good policing.

I could list one hundred of them, but what would you do with a number like that? So assuming there is a reason why there are only Ten Commandments, the Ten Fatal Errors, and only the Top Ten Hits, here are my Ten Myths of Policing.

MYTH 1:
STREET JUSTICE TEACHES PEOPLE A LESSON

This is the kind of perverted reasoning unethical cops use to justify their unlawful use of force. They will argue that when you deal with hardcore criminals you end up fighting a lot. That's pure bs! Most hardcore criminals know they will lose a fight with the cops. They've been there, and they don't usually feel an overwhelming need to get their ass kicked.

But some of us have this need to feel tougher than the bad guy, to prove ourselves. We take advantage of people by pushing their buttons until we get the desired reaction, and then BAMM, we use the maximum force allowable under the law. We get away with it only because the other cops don't report it. We will report that the bad guy started to swing first or he reached into his coat after we told him to keep his hands up. We don't tell you about the verbal taunting that went on prior to the bad guy losing it. We downplay our deliberately aggressive posture or movements that brought the bad guy to a fighting stance.

Everyone knows about the high profile and graphic Rodney King type cases, but we also have many subtle ways to inflict pain, physically and emotionally. For example, not double locking the handcuffs. When the prisoner sits down in the squad car, handcuffed behind the back, the cuffs tighten up against their wrists. The more they struggle to relieve the pressure the worse it gets. Or how about deliberately putting the cuffs on improperly so the prisoner can't get any relief from the pressure? Or having suspects kneel on hot or freezing ground for longer than necessary. There is always the old scam of using snitches (informants) to make arrests and then snitching them off to the very people they informed on. One homicide detective I knew would brag about using a gang member to inform on other gang members and then making the name of his informant known to the gang. His theory was that he got rid of two gang members for the price of one. And, if it produced another murder, so much the better, because then he could start all over again.

Another officer I knew would do whatever he could to shame men in front of their women or peers. Sometimes he left them so angry they were shaking, but then our failure to understand how deeply we anger people is common in police work. Some cops believe they are the law and, if people don't like it, too bad. But when we hurt people unnecessarily or make them lose face in front of others, just because we can, we are making a serious mistake. Some of the people we are so anxious to teach a lesson to are dangerous and violent. When we hurt them or make them lose face for the sole purpose of teaching them a lesson, we create a committed enemy. They will not tolerate being treated like that again, and cops and citizens alike are put at risk when these people strike back. Loss of a sense of honor, or face, can be especially devastating.

Many of these citizens have nothing and they know it. Being on the bottom of the pile economically and socially drives them to fashion an inversely high sense of honor. When we take that away from them with physical force or words of disrespect, we take away the only thing they have left. We create an enemy who has nothing left to lose, except his life or yours.

In *Number Our Days* (1980) Barbara Myerhoff writes about "face":

> The desire to be counted publicly as honorable is certainly a universal human concern. But some societies lavish more care and time on the matter than others. It would seem that there is often a direct, inverse relationship between people's actual effective power and their passion for publicly enacting their honor. Oppressed peoples whose lives are largely determined by forces beyond their control are often preoccupied with "face," and develop subtle gradations of worth and honor in various terms— precise variations in skin color, minor distinctions of dress, and the like. Economic impotence, social inferiority vis-à-vis other groups, removal from centers of authority and influence are among the conditions leading to a great concern with honor. Socially disdained groups have to find their own standards, generating internal codes for taking each other's measure. Only by doing so can they avoid

the devastating consequences of judging themselves in the
terms used by people who disdain them, in whose system
they will always amount to nothing.

This in an incredibly powerful statement about the people cops
deal with the most. Some of these angry people will act out immediately, but some will wait. For the next person who offends them it
can mean a death sentence. A day, a month, or even years later they
will have their revenge. A cop's "lesson" sets up the unknowing
officer, spouse, or boss to be the focal point for an angry and violent
response when the person they were so quick to "educate" finally
explodes. The tough-guy cops who are so busy teaching these lessons might as well be the ones pulling the trigger on the next victim.
Even if they aren't the proximal cause, they can be the last straw.

An officer who worked for me at the academy told me about a
former supervisor who berated him for not beating a juvenile who
ran from a stolen car. When the officer told this supervisor that the
young man gave up after a short foot chase, the supervisor told him
he didn't care. A beating was in order to teach him a lesson, and, if
he ever again caught this officer not hurting someone who ran from
the cops, he would make sure the officer was walking a beat by
himself on nights!

The officer did not change his ways; he continued to do the
right thing. He never reported the supervisor, other than to me. But
what if he had reported the supervisor's comments? There is no
physical evidence to prove his story. The supervisor would deny it,
and the officer becomes a prime candidate for retribution from the

supervisor and his supporters. The Code of Silence protected this supervisor from many legitimate complaints. I testified against him regarding police procedure on a particular case. When it was over, many cops came to me with stories that made me sick at heart over what this cop had gotten away with over the years. The Code of Silence at its finest!

MYTH 2:
THE COURTS WON'T PUNISH PEOPLE
SO THE POLICE MUST

Lots of cops feel it is their duty to punish people. While working as a uniform sergeant, I responded to a call to assist an officer from the Traffic Unit. He needed a female officer to search a woman he believed had stuffed drugs down her blouse on a traffic stop. I ordered a car with a female officer to his location and started over there myself, being curious about the drugs. When I got to his location, he told me he stopped this car with a black male driver and a white female passenger for speeding. The vehicle belonged to the passenger and was registered in her name. The driver gave him a false name and date of birth and claimed he had no id with him. The passenger confirmed the name. The officer determined that the driver was lying about his name because his license was suspended. The female was searched for drugs on a consent search and nothing was found. So far so good.

While waiting for the search to finish, a tow truck arrives and starts hooking up the car. I asked the officer why he was towing the vehicle. "Didn't you tell me it was hers and she had a valid driver's license?" I asked. His response was that it was unit policy to tow cars when drivers lied to the police to "teach them a lesson." I told him, "We don't do that in this precinct," and then ordered him to release the car to the owner. He was so angry and, I assume, embarrassed at being caught, that he let the driver go without charging him. In a memo to this lieutenant he accused me of interfering with his arrest. We ended up in the deputy chief's office where his lieutenant admitted it was their policy to punish people by towing their cars! The good news is the deputy chief put an end to that, I think.

That kind of treatment is frustrating, but just as common and much more disturbing is the physical punishment meted out by cops. Gang members and juveniles are often targeted for special treatment. I've seen cops and their supervisors order kids in gang colors to keep their bare hands on the hood of a car that would have cooked an egg. In the winter I watched officers do the same thing when the temperature was way below zero. I was told—actually the cop was bragging—about one case where a group of bikers were placed face down on the sidewalk, and this cop walked on their hands in his combat boots to show them how tough he was.

I missed the University of Minnesota anti-war riots. It was before my time. But, starting with our first riot control training in 1975, I listened to officers involved in those riots brag about swinging their riot batons like baseball bats at batting practice because "no one could tell who was who in their riot gear." Nine years later I was working in Internal Affairs. A group of angry students made a complaint about being driven around while handcuffed in the back of a police van while the driver alternately slammed on the brakes and made quick accelerations causing the students, handcuffed behind the back, to bounce around off the metal flooring and wooden bench seat. The entire group had bruises and abrasions to show. When questioned, the officer denied any bad driving, claiming he was forced to make several quick stops, the result of heavy traffic. But, after a couple beers, he would freely brag to other cops about bouncing these kids around in the back of the van. Who was this "man among men?" The same riot control trainer who bragged about his swing on previous protesters. The finding, by the way, was "not sustained." There was just his word and his partner's against six young, angry, and bruised kids.

Some cops are good at teaching lessons. Too bad they don't have a clue what they are teaching. Or do they? People who expect to be mistreated are more likely to resist arrest the next time, creating golden opportunities for cops who want to hurt people. It's a lot easier to goad someone who is angry into doing something that will justify an arrest.

MYTH 3:
COPS WHO DEAL WITH A LOT OF BAD GUYS ALWAYS DRAW A LOT MORE COMPLAINTS

This is absolutely not true, but it is used repeatedly by street cops as a defense to complaints of excessive force or abusive language. What is true is that these cops have learned how to push all the right buttons to get a fight started, and they know one-on-one complaints with no witnesses or hard physical evidence will almost always be decided in their favor. I've dealt with a lot of career criminals and sent a lot of them to prison. They don't make complaints any more often than a good citizen.

I supervised the Robbery/Decoy Unit where we targeted active criminals committing crimes against people, and I co-supervised the Repeat Offender Program which targeted the top forty career criminals in Hennepin County. Between those units there were twelve officers who worked on violent and dangerous felons every day for three years. Yet, there was never a complaint of racist language, racial profiling, or excessive force. Not one!

That's not because we were gentle with them. We were forced to be very hard with some, but we were always professional. If they fought, they lost, but there weren't any "lessons taught." Officer K.L. is a good example. She was part of my team when we recovered a murder weapon on a search warrant in a really nasty biker bar. During the search, a drunk pulled a knife and attempted to cut her throat. It would have been a legally justified use of deadly force, and most cops would have shot this dummy. What did she do? In one move she took away his knife and threw him to the floor on his back. Then she berated him for being so stupid! And she did it all before we could move to help her. Later that night we teased her about leaving this moron in the gene pool, but we didn't push it too hard. What she did was brave and smart.

Don't get the impression I advocate being gentle with criminals. The officers I worked with were as tough as they come when they had to be, but when the fight was over it was over. We did what we had to do, not what we could do. Not that I didn't lose my temper on occasion.

One really hot night we set up a robbery decoy in a very high-crime area where there was a real mix of people with only one thing in common—poverty. Our decoy was sitting on a retaining wall outside a bar when he was approached by two vicious and notorious criminals. When a big Indian man tried to step in and stop the two thieves from taking the decoy's watch and money, they each punched him in the face. We moved in to arrest them and ended up chasing them on foot. The one I was chasing ran for blocks and, at one point, ran right through the middle of an outdoor barbecue party. Someone at the party did not want me to catch him. As I ran by she took a baseball swing with a beer bottle and hit me on the end of my nose. My face felt like it exploded and blood ran everywhere. I stumbled but kept running. The officer behind me saw what happened to me and, to avoid the same fate, knocked her to the ground as he ran by.

About three blocks later my bad guy goes over a high fence into a yard with a lot of bushes, and I lose sight of him. I run around to the other side of the house, but he doesn't come out of the yard. By now several uniformed cars are at the scene, and one is a K9 car. He takes his dog through the yard and searches for the suspect. My face, in the meantime, is swelling up like a balloon, and I get several suggestions to go to the emergency room. There is blood running down my throat, and it's making me sick to my stomach.

The K9 officer comes out of the yard and tells me the guy must have gotten away because the dog never indicated on anything in the yard. Now I am really angry. But all is not lost. My friends and former partners Don and Ted are there, and they ask me if I am sure the bad guy is still in the yard. I tell them I am sure, and they say, "OK we'll search it." They don't go more than twenty feet around the house before there is a lot of commotion and yelling.

Next thing I know they are walking out with my bad guy, covered in dirt from hiding deep in the shrubbery next to the house. The K9 had literally walked over the top of the bad guy and never indicated to his handler he was there. My anger gets the best of me. I grab this dirt-covered excuse for a human being by the throat and lift him off the ground against the side of the house. Ted and Don firmly take each of my arms and quietly say, "That's enough Mike, you got him." That is what real partners and great cops do when another cop steps over the line. We went back to find the woman who hit me in the nose, but the entire house and yard were empty. They even left their food cooking on the grill. Apparently they didn't want to talk to us.

Any cop who tells you they are getting lots of complaints solely because the people they are dealing with are hardened criminals is a liar, plain and simple. Every cop will draw some complaints about language or excessive force in their career. But only a few cops continue to generate the same complaints and lawsuits over and over. They are abusing people. You may not ever be able to "prove" it, but that is what they are doing.

MYTH 4:
SWEARING AND CURSING
ARE NECESSARY IN POLICE WORK

At one time I believed this myself. I even drafted a memo to the chief about cursing to shock people and get their attention when they are out of control. I've learned over the years that I was wrong, very wrong. There is incredible power in words. Words evoke feelings in you and the person you are directing them toward. Good investigators learn this and use the right words to get voluntary confessions or admissions. Good street cops do the same to de-escalate situations. But some cops use swearing and cursing just to make people angry.

What we don't realize is that our own anger is fueled by the use of inflammatory words. It interferes with our thinking and clouds our judgment. This is really bad news for cops. In a crisis situation we need to think clearly and be as unemotional as possible. Using swear words and cursing arouses the feelings associated with those words in ourselves and the people they are directed toward. The angrier we are the higher the adrenaline flows. The higher the adrenaline flows the less the reasoning brain can function. In terms of officer survival, cops can't afford to lose any control of rational thought. So, if we know that, why do we do it? Do we really want people out of control? Smart cops don't, but for an unethical cop it certainly makes some people easier to arrest, doesn't it? And, better yet, angry people often respond physically, creating a need for the officer to use force to control the situation. What a deal. It's another two-for-one thing.

MYTH 5:
USE OF RACIAL OR OTHER DEROGATORY SLURS IS OK AS LONG AS IT IS NOT ON THE JOB

Even unspoken words evoke feelings, and feelings will bring out the words associated with them. When we think in derogatory terms, even without speaking them, we bring up the feelings associated with those terms. Nigger, Spic, Fag, Dyke, Dogeater, Slant Eyes, whatever the terms, if we use them, even if we just think them, our behavior will be a reflection of what is going on in our head.

You will hear police supervisors say they can't tell cops how to feel about issues like race or sexual preference. They will tell you that it is ok to be racist in private as long as you don't show it on the job. Maybe we can't dictate feelings, but feelings or words loaded with hate, prejudice, or stereotypes carry with them predetermined value judgments that carry over to the statements, interrogations, and other evidence we evaluate. They create a subconscious smoke screen that prevents otherwise good cops from making an honest and critical evaluation of people and/or evidence.

It feeds into the attitude of cops "knowing" what happened or "knowing" who did it. And for a cop that can be fatal. Look at the people wrongfully convicted. I am willing to bet that, in a number of those cases, a cop decided who was guilty before all the evidence was recovered or there was evidence of innocence that was discounted. Eliminating prejudicial, racist, or sexist words from your vocabulary isn't just about being politically correct. It is about having a clear mind, free of obstructions, that allows you to make smart, maybe even life-saving, decisions. Ultimately, it is about officer safety for you and your partners.

MYTH 6:
ONCE YOU ARE IN THE CODE OF SILENCE GROUP, YOU CAN'T GET OUT

The Code is not a pass/fail exam that you take only once. We are who we are by the choices we continue to make, not just the bad choices we made in the past. A bad decision or mistake that is identified as such can be used to improve performance and will make a better cop. Good choices go a long way toward making up for bad decisions, and they are a lot less stressful.

I didn't make all the right decisions in my career. I've done things I shouldn't, and I've let my anger get the best of me. Whenever I've shared stories about my own shameful acts with other cops, I find that we are all in the same boat. We all struggle with integrity issues and the Code of Silence. The difference is that the men and women who really want to make a difference are willing to wage war against the Code of Silence. They know they will lose some of those battles on both a personal and a professional level. Still, your best cops will try every day to do this job the way the public expects and deserves. Sometimes they will fail. That doesn't make them failures, bound to the Code. It just means they're human. Making a mistake or doing something stupid may be hard to admit. It may even be embarrassing. But it's the job we signed up to do. Life is messy, and police work is all about cleaning up the mess. And we all make mistakes.

I once pulled my gun to arrest a drug dealer in a very crowded fast-food restaurant. I let the gun get too close to the suspect and I ended up fighting for my life. We both had our hands on the gun, but the suspect had control of it. He pointed it into my belly with his thumb pushing against the trigger as we spun around through a crowd of screaming panicked patrons. Only my grip on the hammer and cylinder kept him from killing me or a customer. Only my partner, Don, kept me from being killed when he took the suspect down from behind. I learned a lot from that mistake and did not repeat it. But I made others.

My ego really got the best of me on one occasion. My partner and I were assigned to provide security for Secretary of the Interior James Watt at a local hotel. We were in a marked squad in full uniform. I parked on the newly-tiled sidewalk in front of the hotel because there was nowhere else to park. As I got out of the car, a construction worker started screaming obscenities at me for parking on his sidewalk. My blood came to full boil immediately. We were ordered to go directly into the hotel by the dispatcher, but when the security detail was over I went straight to the construction worker. We exchanged some words. He got mad. I got madder. A struggle ensued, and he went to jail. To make a long story short my partner and I were sued for excessive force and civil rights violations. It was a justifiable arrest, just not a very smart one.

A judge told me later that if we had charged this guy with "obscenities in public" instead of "disorderly conduct" there never would have been a lawsuit. Even the chief of police supported us by saying, "It's not what I would have done, but I understand how it happened." My partner and I were tried in civil court. Words are not adequate to explain how horrible it feels when the jury foreman says, "We find the defendants 'guilty.'" The verdict was eventually vacated, and the city settled for $13,000. I vowed it would never happen again, and it didn't. I wasn't wrong legally in what I did, but clearly I had stepped outside the community's expectations of police conduct and they let us know it.

There is no way to list every possible or even probable mistake a cop will make. The mistakes of letting someone lie for you or you lying to cover for someone else are almost inevitable, but they can be a learning experience. For each cop there will be different experiences, and for each cop individual decisions—some easy, some gut wrenching. We should forgive cops for real mistakes but we must also hold them accountable. We have cops who are repeatedly accused of excessive force and abusive language. These cops are abusing people, make no mistake. Instead of holding them accountable, though, we stick with an old system that rewards these cops for their actions by telling the public there isn't enough evidence to convict them. Chief law enforcement officers who use this reasoning with cops who get repeated complaints are doing a disservice to the community and the department.

Minneapolis had a new officer who received so many "use of force" complaints in his first year that the administration pulled him off the street. What did they do with him? Rather than fire him, which would have been easy, and smart, they rewarded him by sending him to an instructor's school for the use of force so he could teach other Minneapolis cops how to use force! You have to wonder what the chief was thinking on that one!

MYTH 7:
TOUGHER LAW ENFORCEMENT IS THE ANSWER

Tougher enforcement of the law is a two-edged sword. In Hennepin County, for instance, we can continue the current course of action and we will create a criminal record for every black male between the ages of 18 and 30.

Minneapolis lies completely within the boundaries of Hennepin County and the November 2000 Hennepin County African American Men Project Report illustrates the devastating side effects crack cocaine distribution and the resulting crime reduction efforts can have when the police take the time to exert their full power.

The report found that nearly half the African American men ages 18–30 in Hennepin County had arrest records. This is in conjunction with a legal system in Minnesota that incarcerates Blacks 26.8 times more often than whites, the worst racial disparity in the 50 States. (Human Rights Watch, 1999)

We will probably show a reduction in the use and sale of crack cocaine. There will be a lot of women and kids with no husbands or fathers in their lives. There will be a lot of men with a criminal history that bars them from anything but menial jobs, so they are bound to go back to criminal activities as a way to make money. We will need bigger jails and more prisons because we are running out of room already. Where, exactly, is this drug war taking us? During prohibition, cops killed men just for selling and transporting liquor. The enforcement of the prohibition laws created some of the largest criminal enterprises in the world. Now the "drug war" is creating criminal kingdoms that make Al Capone look like the "Mister Rogers of Crime." Anybody else see a problem here?

Tougher law enforcement and a policy of "convict and incarcerate" is not the answer. Each and every action a cop takes creates a ripple effect that moves through the entire community, and we can no longer deny responsibility for the foreseeable outcome of a policy that did not work during prohibition and is not working in the drug war. To do so is like pulling the trigger and denying responsibility for where the bullet strikes. We cops see what is happening on the streets. We are in a better position than anyone in the criminal justice system to determine what we should be doing. We can no longer hide behind the old argument, "We don't make the laws, we just enforce them." When it comes to enforcing the law, we have discretionary power second to none. We demean ourselves and our profession when we choose to ignore the devastating effects of a policy of "convict and incarcerate."

McNamara's survey is a wake-up call for legislators and law enforcement around the world. Ninety percent of the cops he surveyed said increased prevention and treatment could control drugs more effectively. Across the nation, criminal justice agencies have taken the first step in analyzing crime statistics to determine a proper course of crime and drug control. We need to take the next critical step and analyze what we are doing to our communities of color. We are not now and never will be the only answer to the crime problem.

MYTH 8:
LEADERSHIP MEANS YOU HAVE TO BE PROMOTED AND BE THE TOUGHEST SOB ON THE SHIFT

Leadership is as much a state of mind as it is a position of appointed authority. Treating people with dignity, respecting the rights of others, and communicating in a thoughtful manner with victims and suspects alike is as much a demonstration of leadership as any rank worn on the uniform. Plus, it is well known that some of the strongest leadership in a law enforcement agency comes from its informal leaders, not its promoted personnel. These are the cops who arouse other officers' passions about issues, and they have a lot of power. In his book *Leading Minds: An Anatomy of Leadership (1995, 48)* Howard Gardner explains it this way:

> Social psychologists have shown repeatedly that the pres-
> tige of a spokesperson, the identities of a speaker's friends
> and enemies, and the exploitation of nostalgia or griev-
> ances more strongly shape attitudinal change than the
> sheer merits of rational argument do.

When it comes down to it, the argument that carries the
day may well be the one that exerts the strongest affective appeal, rather than the one that triumphs on debating
points.

Here we can see the power of the Code when it is endorsed by
a strong informal leader. It has great affective appeal—the common
enemy is the human predator preying on innocent citizens, and the
Code gives us the power we want to deal with our enemy. Conversely, to step outside the Code, to do things the right way, requires
much more effort and more courage than a lot of us can muster.
Not that cops are short on courage; the majority of cops are capable
of heroic acts in the face of danger. The courage I am talking about
comes out of a core value system that honors "protect and serve."
Courage that supports telling the truth, even when it hurts.

It's doing the right thing when no one is watching that's tough. (Sgt.
Warren Ackerson)

In *Working with Emotional Intelligence* (1998, 188), Goleman
quotes a U.S. Navy study on leaders that really hits home about the
kind of skills we should be trying to develop in our cops.

In an extensive comparison of superior and just average
commands, a striking difference in the emotional tone the
commanding officers set was revealed. The very best commands, it turned out, were run not by Captain Ahab types
who terrorized their crews, but by, well . . . nice guys.

The superior leaders managed to balance a people-ori-
ented personal style with a decisive command role. They

did not hesitate to take charge, to be purposeful, assertive, and businesslike. But the greatest difference between average and superior leaders was in their emotional style. The most effective leaders were more positive and outgoing, more emotionally expressive and dramatic, warmer and more sociable (including smiling more), friendlier and more democratic, more cooperative, more likeable and "fun to be with," more appreciative and trustful, and even gentler than those who were merely average.

By contrast, the mediocre navy leaders reflected the classic stereotype of the military taskmaster. They were legalistic, negative, harsh, disapproving, and egocentric.

Compared to the superior commanders, the average ones were more authoritarian and controlling, more domineering and tough-minded, more aloof and self-centered, and needed to show they were right more often. They led by the book, through the rules and assertion of the raw power of their position.

And it did not work, even in the military, where this emotional style might seem to find its natural home.

And it doesn't work in police training or supervision either!

MYTH 9:
PEOPLE ONLY RESPECT WHAT THEY FEAR

Fear is about as far from respect as hate is from love, but cops use this reasoning all the time to justify black leather "gun fighter" gloves, mirrored sun glasses, rough language, etc. People avoid those they fear. They may obey them when they are present, but they put their obedience away as soon as those they fear are out of sight.

A former academy supervisor spent a great deal of time one day telling me how important it was for the recruits to fear the instructors. He told me several things he did during the academy to embarrass and generate real fear in the recruits. It struck me as sad how little this guy knew about people and training. The really awful part is that he trained a lot of cops to treat people the same way he treated the recruits. Some of those recruits became field training officers for the recruits I was putting through the academy. The Code of Silence was at the very core of his teaching, and he used it to create fear in people, but he never understood respect.

Of course, a lot of cops have been trained in the "fear" method. They will use inflammatory language and physical appearance to create a sense of dread in the people they deal with because their trainers used that approach whenever they dealt with them. If you want to see what kind of cops you will have in your community, take a close look at their training program. The behavior modeled by the trainers is the behavior the recruits will exhibit on the street. Look very closely at the first few days of training and anything labeled "stress training." If there is a lot of yelling and screaming and the trainers spend a lot of time trying to embarrass or anger the recruits, that is exactly what those recruits will do to the citizens they deal with. Not all of them of course. Some will see through the BS. But they will be in the minority.

Real stress training creates men and women who see yelling and screaming as a loss of control, not a way to get control. Real stress training produces cops who are stronger than they look. Cops who have the self-confidence and inner strength to do what needs to be done in the most trying and dangerous circumstances. Cops who are not afraid of the Code. Cops who grow stronger from their battles with Code, both won and lost.

MYTH 10:
YOU NEED TO BE MACHO TO BE A GOOD COP

A female deputy, a former student of mine, had been working for a local county sheriff's office. She was the only female on the department working on road patrol. I knew her to be smart and a critical thinker. As she finished her probation, she was told she was being fired.

The reason given by the sheriff was that "she just wasn't working out." She was reinstated a short time later. She asked to work on road patrol and was immediately put on administrative leave while the sheriff tried to justify firing her. He couldn't! Now she's back to work full time, but there are still *no* women working road patrol in that county.

Women cops do the job differently than male cops. They have to. Their genes have set them up with smaller muscle mass while, with few exceptions, our police training has set them up with tactics that only work well for people (read men) with more muscle mass. Either way, they are set up from the beginning because female cops are still being judged by male standards and they are asked to the job with training that favors the male physique. To help lessen the blow, I always told the female recruits, "If you don't do the job better than a man doing the same job you will be seen as not doing it as well." This always angered some of our macho cops. They complain about the way women cops work because they don't do the job the same way men do. They argue that the job is the same for every cop, regardless of size or gender. That is a true statement, as far as it goes. But it's only part of the story.

Cops use physical force on the job less than five percent of the time, and every cop I know does this job a little differently. I know some very macho cops, legends in their own minds, who are such poor physical specimens they couldn't fight their way out of a roll of wet toilet paper. They are the epitome of the phrase "an alligator mouth with a hummingbird ass." I never heard anyone criticize them. But then why would they? They were men. And I know big physically powerful macho cops who never learned decent communication skills because they always got by on their brawn. Of course, they are always the first ones to complain that women cops spend too much time trying to communicate with people.

Physical and mental fitness is an essential element of officer survival, but cops don't need to be big, macho, and super strong to be successful. In every academy class I supervised, which totaled almost 300 new officers over four years, there was always a macho attitude in the first few weeks, the result of an overabundance of testosterone, and too many cop reality shows.

I could usually capitalize on an incident or event in training to show the class how little importance should be placed on whether a cop is male or female. In one class I had a recruit who believed that to be a cop in Minneapolis you had to be over six feet tall, *male*, and very strong. I'm pretty sure he picked this up from some of the part-time instructors at the academy. When he began making his beliefs known to the women and smaller men in the class, word got back to me very quickly.

The cadre officers at the academy wanted me to confront this recruit, but I liked him and I saw great potential. Besides, I didn't want him angry. I wanted him smart and successful. I asked the cadre officer in charge of the class to get the six best runners from the class and have them fall out with me for physical training the next morning. It was cold that day. There was at least a foot of new snow on the ground, and the temp must have been around 15° Fahrenheit. Everyone formed up outside for a run called "The Grinder," a three-mile run with twenty pushups and twenty sit-ups every half mile.

The six fell in with me. Then I told our macho man he would be running with us. He was a big guy, over six feet, and about 250 pounds. He may have been a sprinter, but he was definitely not a distance runner. We took off at an easy nine minute/mile pace and at half a mile we dropped in the snow to do twenty pushups and twenty situps. Macho Man had stayed with us, but he was clearly hurting. He began losing ground as soon as we got up and started running again.

I did not allow any negative comments about his inability to keep up. I made sure the other recruits running with me understood we were to give him only positive support. Every half mile for the next four miles we stopped and did pushups and situps, and each time Macho Man was unable to do them with us because he was too far behind. So we would circle back, and then run with him at his pace up to the point where we had done the pushups and situps, and then we would all do them again with him. We provided constant reinforcement throughout the run telling him we were there for him, that we wouldn't leave him, and we wouldn't let him fail—no matter what.

As we approached the academy and the end of the drill, Macho Man was unable to do a single pushup, even though he had done only half as many as his fellow recruits. I sent the others ahead at the last half mile and I walked in with our now Less-than-Macho Man. I asked if he knew what the workout was about. He told me he pretty much figured it out when he saw who he was lined up with to run.

I know this was probably the toughest workout of his life, but he never quit, and he never complained, even when he found himself unable to do what everyone else was doing. He pushed himself to new limits, but not out of fear, out of pride. This remediated recruit became one of the most supportive and motivating men who had ever come through the academy. At a recruit graduation he attended, after he had been on the street for some time, he told me that the lesson he learned that day was the most important of the entire academy.

This example of the macho attitude was easy to see because our macho man was big and male. But macho is really about attitude, not just size and gender. I know many women cops and smaller male cops who come across with the same macho attitude this young recruit displayed. To hear them talk, they are the toughest cops in the city. Of course, most of them are anything but.

Physical strength is just one issue. Policing isn't always about strength, and women are better at some police jobs than men. I'll give you an example. If I have to choose between a woman and a man for a partner to do undercover work, I will always choose a woman. Two men together in plain clothes might as well have "police" tattooed on their foreheads unless they are willing to play gay partners. That works in a limited number of places and most straight cops wouldn't or couldn't pull it off. But a man and woman together can devise all sorts of scenarios to fit in anywhere; and a female officer who is good looking with some street smarts will get unsolicited admissions and confessions from male criminals who let their gonads do their speaking for them.

Don't tell me women can't do this job. Any cop who says that just isn't smart enough to do the job with anything but his muscles and his cojones. The majority of police work is about communication, not physical force. It occurs to me that women are often more adept at crisis communication than men. Makes you wonder which gender will be the minority in the future of policing, doesn't it?

Now What Do We Do?

Our answer must consist, not in talk and meditation, but in right action and in right conduct. Life ultimately means taking the responsibility to find the right answer to its problems and to fulfill the tasks which it constantly sets for each individual.

VIKTOR FRANKL 1905–1997

THE POLICE CHIEF AND PLAUSIBLE DENIABILITY

IN ITS NOVEMBER 2003 EDITION, *The Police Chief* magazine carried an article by Craig E. Ferrell Jr., Deputy Director, Administrative General Counsel, Houston Police Department, Houston, Texas. In the article Ferrell argues that there is no Code of Silence, that it is only a myth perpetuated upon the public by the movie makers. Ferrell claims that, "Proper training and supervision will create an environment that will not tolerate corruption and misconduct and that will take proactive steps to eliminate it when it occurs."

Recent news accounts about the Houston cops tell me that Ferrell should reconsider his position.

> January, 2004. The Houston Police Department badge
> has lost some of its luster recently. The Kmart raid, the
> shootings of two teenage boys, and the charging of five
> officers with shaking down cantinas for protection are
> among events that have raised questions about how HPD
> has been run. Now, Mayor Bill White is looking for a new
> police chief. (www.Click2Houston.com)

Ferrell closes his article by saying, "Dispelling the myth of a code of silence is not a simple or quick task. Just like I always tell my children, trust is something that takes a lifetime to achieve but only seconds to destroy. Through proper training, proactive supervision, and open communication with the public, we can gain the public's trust and confidence, and convince them that a code of silence exits only in the movies."

I think Deputy Director Ferrell, Jr., is right in what he wants to accomplish, and his goals are admirable. But, when the people advising our top cops deny the existence of the Code they do a disservice to the community, the cops, and themselves. The Code of Silence is not a myth and "proper training" must include discussion of the Code and the tough decisions cops will have to make regarding the conduct of other cops.

"Proactive supervision" should include training supervisors on how to deal with cops who revert to the Code for protection.

"Open communication" should include telling the community how the Code works, why cops buy into it, and what good cops are doing to try and avoid it.

But, to deny its existence, in *The Police Chief* magazine? We're only fooling ourselves. Instead of opening communication with the public, we are shutting them off. They know better. They've seen the Code in action, and I'd be willing to bet that a number of Houston's citizens will look at Ferrell's statements as just one more lie to cover for bad cops. I would also be willing to bet he was trying to do just the opposite.

There are lots of good cops.

Many good cops take leadership roles in their organization and their community. They are working hard to make us the profession the public expects and deserves.They warrant the support of their communities. But there are far too many of us operating like combatants in a war on crime and drugs. Too few who see themselves as Peace Officers and part of a community effort. Even with the strong focus on community policing, cops in many cities have abandoned their community partners. Instead, they are abiding by the Code and turning their backs on the very people they profess to be helping. We have gone down the wrong road and we need to find our way back. We need to get back to doing "for the people" not "to the people."

The following is from Robert McNamara's essay "America's Plague of Bad Cops." (McNamara Collection, Shaffer Library of Drug Policy)

True, American policing has greatly improved since the civil rights movement directed attention to police abuses. But the recent outbreak of bad-cop problems has cost police forces a lot of the credibility we had gained among minority groups with good policing. Still. There is one silver lining in the cloud of distrust created by the Fuhrman tapes and the plethora of police scandals: more self-scrutiny.

We should not, however, make the mistake of getting lost in debates about such reform mechanisms as civilian-review boards, community policing and special prosecutors. Rather, the essential task is to create within police agencies an incentive to break the code of silence among the rank and file and encourage cops to police themselves. A corrupt, racist or brutal cop will abstain from misconduct only when he looks at the cop next to him and believes that the officer will -blow the whistle if he hits the suspect.

The police value system is what permits the kind of behavior that gets bad headlines. Real reform is possible only when that value system changes and cops come to realize that they must police themselves.

My own experience is that reporting police misconduct is risky, at best. And we can look at the example set here with Officer Keith Batt in Oakland, California.

Dec. 9, 2003. (BCN)—The three former Oakland police officers charged with illegal conduct in the so-called

"Riders" case won't be riding off into the sunset any time soon, as prosecutors today filed amended charges that they think will have a better chance of winning convictions.

The former officers' first trial on allegations that they conspired to beat and frame suspected drug dealers in West Oakland lasted over a year and ended on Sept. 30 with jurors acquitting the defendants on eight counts and deadlocking on the remaining 27 counts.
(KGT-TV/DT San Francisco)

THE FUTURE OF CRIMINAL JUSTICE ETHICS TRAINING

Since I wrote and published *Walking With the Devil: The Police Code of Silence* in 2005, I have received numerous letters and emails from officers across Canada and the United States with stories similar to mine. They are men and women who told the truth to commanders, supervisors, or IA investigators about misconduct they witnessed, and they were ignored, told to keep quiet, shunned, labeled a rat, or forced to change careers. The following emails from November of 2009 are an example of what is happening to officers and constables across North America.

> Mr. Quinn, I am a Canadian police officer. I have read your book with great interest and suddenly do not feel so alone. I'm glad that somebody has written about a topic that is so often viewed as the "elephant in the room" that no one wants to talk about.

Three years ago, I, along with eight other police officers from my police force, witnessed a senior constable kick a handcuffed, prone prisoner in the head. This constable was out of control and had been for quite some time. Out of all the police officers present during the incident, I was the only one who reported the assault to a superior non-commissioned officer. He, in turn, told me to tell another, more senior NCO. That NCO chose to bury the incident which, in the end, made things worse as the incident was reported anonymously to the Police Complaints Commission. Needless to say the constable in question was charged with assault causing bodily harm, one NCO had to resign and the more superior NCO was disciplined for deceit. I have had to testify five separate times with respect to this incident during internal and external investigations, a coroner's inquest and court. Everyone at my department knows what I did.

I know I did the right thing, but I'm struggling. My department has basically left me to "twist in the wind." I feel like an outcast, and it's very clear that I will not be promoted because of this incident. I have gone over the incident a thousand times in my head, and I know I would not change a thing that I did, and that does give me some peace of mind. I was just wondering whether you knew of any other good books on this topic?

Thanks for your consideration,

A Canadian Officer (Name withheld to protect the privacy of the officer. Edited for clarity)

Here is another one.

Mr. Quinn,

Your book "The Police Code of Silence Walking with the
Devil" was suggested to me by a friend as an excellent
example of police officers deciding to break the "Blue
Code of Silence" as I decided to make that choice in
November of 2007.

I have been an officer for over ten years and received
all the training you spoke about in your book, both in
the Academy and after, regarding ethics, report writing, street training vs. academy training, and so forth.
As you stated, the instructors have always verbally told
us to be honest in our reports and in court. That if you
see an officer do something wrong you must report it or
you're just as at fault. I remember one of my Oral Board
Questions was "You walk into your sergeant's office and
catch him/her drinking while on duty, What do you do?"
The answer they want to hear is "Tell your sergeant. You
saw what they were doing, and you would go with them
to turn themselves in or you would have to do it, because
lives were in jeopardy when they were drinking on the
job, both driving and carrying a gun." Now, once you hit
the street "Cops don't tell on other cops. Not for any reason. Ever!"

As you clearly stated in your book, that is made clear
pretty much from the moment you hit the streets. I think
officers are also tested on that "Code of Silence" when
they start as well. I was on a call with a sergeant during
field training when after we got the subject arrested and

in the back of the patrol vehicle, he punched the guy in the face because of name calling. Right after he did that, both my FTO and the sergeant looked at me and said "You didn't see a thing." I was stunned by the action and the comment. The suspect never made a complaint to Internal Affairs that I knew about, but to this day I feel horrible for not protecting that person even though he was a suspect. That sergeant is known for behavior like that and keeps a tight group of people around him, and I was happy never to have to permanently work his shift.

I will try to make this short. In November 2007 I made that dreaded choice and went to Internal Affairs, crossing the "Thin Blue Line," and turned in an officer for wrong-doing against two fellow officers and my husband and me. This also included officer safety issues. I had followed my original answer to the oral board somewhat because before I went I told the officer that what he was saying was wrong but his actions continued. Going to Internal Affairs was a gut-wrenching experience and something I hoped I would never have to do. I kept the fact that I went to IA secret from everyone, including my husband (who also works for the department,) because of the stigma that goes with being a "Rat."

Against all the rules of IA they failed to keep the fact that I had gone in secrecy and told the officer that I made a complaint. As you can imagine it started a domino effect that is still ongoing. My husband was threatened by the officer and told basically to keep his wife's mouth shut; he started getting write-ups and ignored on his shift; IA complaints were made up about it; and he was "passed over" for a special assignment after this officer (who happened to be his sergeant) provided false information to the special assignment sergeant (this was later learned); and he was given a bad evaluation for the first time in his ten-year career.

I was removed from my special assignment, my work locker was broken into, payroll was messed with and my locker filled with trash. I received IA complaints by this officer after he was moved into my special assignment area as a sergeant and I was written up for stuff like going to an IA interview; sergeant claiming he didn't know, even though he got the email. I was given my first bad evaluation in ten years, however, it was six months late, and they couldn't provide documentation to go with it.

For all accounts both my husband and I were considered excellent officers with good moral characters. We both had several commendation letters from citizens and excellent reviews. We were allowed to attend almost any training class we wanted, and we were often chosen for special assignments.

IA never conducted an investigation regarding my complaints. However, they allowed the officer I complained about to file a complaint in January 2008 against the two other officers. Both my husband and I were required to attend a taped IA interview in March 2008 (at different times) during which time I complained about persons running me through NCIC, and we provided information on the other officers that they didn't want to hear. Our IA tapes disappeared, and we were later told by Human Resources that they were erased because they weren't needed, according to IA, although our laws and policy state everything must be retained.

We have had persons try to break into our home, and neighbors (whom I didn't know at the time) witnessed people in the back of our house shining very bright flashlights into our home from the back yard and then they saw people running when I came out to clear the house.

After making enough complaints about the treatment, missing IA tapes, NCIC use, and the fact that I felt unsafe at work, the police chief and the director of HR directed a lieutenant to conduct a special investigation that was supposed to be kept "Hush Hush." Well, that Lt. conducted the investigation but then shared the information with witnesses and suspect officers and recently left the department for "early retirement." I was told that the investigation was compromised and had to be redone but not who redid it.

In the meantime, an unknown person mailed a letter to officers private homes and City Council Members' homes telling them in no uncertain terms I was a "Rat." The City and the Police Department failed to notify me about the letter, but members of my department confronted me. Lucky for me someone turned a copy of it into the union so I was able to read it. When I confronted the chief, I was advised they had a copy but didn't feel the need to notify me because they didn't know who wrote it, but they did send out an email telling people to stop spreading rumors. They conducted no investigation and felt it didn't put me in harm's way.

Both my husband and I have sat in meetings with the

director of human resources and explained to him that we felt unsafe because everything has been compromised from the investigation and that officers would go to great lengths to keep other officers mouths shut. We were worried about being on a call for service and requesting back up and getting none. The director said he didn't believe that would happen and that we were overreacting to the situation. The "Hush Hush" investigation, which I have been told is completed now (but have never been given a copy,) was turned over to IA. Several of the suspect officers still work there, so now they know even more of what we told them. I remember getting very mad at the HR director at the time and telling him if he was going to be working with a police department he needed to take a class on police retaliation and the "Code Of Silence" so he could understand where we were coming from.

When I tell people this story (and you're only getting a small part), I feel like I am telling them something from a movie script and it's not really my life. It has affected the lives of my family, husband, dear friends, my health and my belief in what the "badge" is supposed to stand for. The quote you wrote in your book summoned up a lot of what is going on with me and some of the other officers involved in this case. "The pervasiveness of the code of silence is bolstered by the grave consequences for violating it: Officers who report misconduct are ostracized and harassed; become targets of complaints and even physical threats; and are made to fear that we will be left alone on the streets in a time of crisis." (Mollen 1994, 53) from pg 35

It upsets me that the "bad apples" involved in this mess are still able to walk around and do whatever they want, and that all of a sudden our integrity was being questioned. Although I know what I did was right and had to be done with the knowledge I have now, I would have done things a little differently to keep them from getting away with what they did. It makes me wonder if they are doing this to one of their own what are they doing to those citizens on the street who don't [know] any different.

I want to thank you for writing this book, and I wish there were more like it for those of us who have or who will decide to make the choice to cross the "Thin Blue Line."

A Canadian Officer, (Name withheld to protect the privacy of the officer)

I believe in my heart that most cops want to be honest with the public and themselves. Years of shared stories and experiences with officers from all over the world have shown me this is true. But, even with the best of intentions, we sometimes stumble and violate the oath we took to be peace officers. Asking cops to report misconduct is like asking the public to write themselves traffic citations. It happens, but not often enough.

A great example of what *is* possible comes out of Princeton, West Virginia, where Lt. Compton, Sergeant Ruble and Officer Gergely sued their own department, broke the code of silence and won. Was there a cost? Certainly, but here is a short piece from an email I received from Lt. Compton.

> . . . I have participated in the code but finally could not take it any longer, and Officer Gergely, Sergeant Ruble and myself finally crossed the line and now are the bad guys among the local departments and officers. I do not regret for one second what we did and just wanted to let you know. . . .

Maybe they are the "bad guys" for now, but you can't put a price on personal integrity. The fact that these brave officers had the integrity and the guts to do the right thing is just one more proof that the vast majority of cops are good cops who want to do this job the right way. So what stops them? The code of silence for one, but it's not the only thing standing in their way. There is a real lack of support from administrators for officers who are willing to come forward with complaints. Following is a recent example.

The Minnesota Gang Strike Force

This once highly respected unit has been shut down, and some officers are facing criminal charges for gross misconduct. A former supervisor has resigned for alleged misconduct. One officer was fired for Strike Force misconduct and the office manager has been fired from the sheriff's office.

Here is a short piece from the Luger/Egelhof report of the Strike Force investigation that was presented in August of 2009.

> Our respect for law enforcement cannot change the ines-capable conclusion that a great deal went wrong at the Metro Gang Strike Force. Based on our experience and as

a result of our investigation, we have reached the conclusion that some of the individuals at the Metro Gang Strike
Force engaged in serious misconduct, misconduct that
was appalling and outrageous. Our Report condemns
their actions.

While this is a sad day for all who have faith in and
trust law enforcement, our Report is not a criticism of law
enforcement in general. As I will discuss this morning,
something went terribly wrong at the Metro Gang Strike
Force. And it must never happen again.

At the same time, many Strike Force officers worked
hard, followed the law and conducted appropriate investigations that make all of us more safe.[9]

We know from the information that has come out about the
investigation that there was distrust within the unit. Some cops were
following the rules while others were allegedly illegally seizing,
keeping or selling property they obtained during arrests. Twelve
cops are being investigated. That's a third of the Strike Force officers.
So why didn't the good cops report what was going on?

One possible reason is that they saw what happened to Sergeant Kelly O'Rourke when a year earlier he reported the misconduct to his lieutenant, Jim Heimerl, who is now allegedly at the
center of the investigation. O'Rourke was transferred off the unit, a
"lateral demotion." He didn't know about Heimerl's involvement
in the misconduct. On the upside, O'Rourke sued the department
over the transfer and he won. Here is the Minneapolis Star Tribune
report of what happened.

MINNEAPOLIS SETTLES WITH POLICE SERGEANT
OVER GANG STRIKE FORCE SUIT

A settlement has been reached in a whistle-blower case involving a Minneapolis police sergeant who claimed he was removed from the Metro Gang Strike Force after voicing concerns about its actions.

On Friday, the City Council voted, 11–0, to pay $12,500 to the League of Minnesota Cities Insurance Trust as part of an $80,000 settlement agreement between the trust and police Sergeant. Kelly O'Rourke.

Last year, O'Rourke sued the city of Minneapolis alleging he was transferred back from the Strike Force to the Police Department after warning city supervisors in 2007 about what he deemed to be improper evidence handling by the now-disbanded Strike Force.

He also accused unnamed officers of carrying out a campaign of retaliation that included leaking his name to news media in a report claiming O'Rourke had used an ice auger seized by the Strike Force.

His attorney, Patrick Burns, said then that "any allegation against Sergeant. O'Rourke is patently false." He noted, too, that O'Rourke was working undercover at the time the lawsuit was filed, which the department wouldn't allow, he said, if it had concerns about his police work. Burns could not be reached to comment Friday night.

Late Friday afternoon, City Attorney Susan Segal said that the $80,000 settlement was negotiated by the League of Minnesota Cities Insurance Trust, and that "we participated to get the thing done."

The City Council approved the $12,500 payment after meeting in a closed executive session.[10]

O'Rourke deserves a lot of credit for coming forward. He had to know what would happen when he did, but O'Rourke is not the only officer out there with the guts to report misconduct.

He is one of a growing number of good cops saying "Not Here. Not Now. Not in Front of Me!"

The following news article from Houston, Texas is another example of cops doing the right thing.

POLICE SERGEANT'S COMMENTS OF ARRESTING, BEATING PEOPLE AT HOUSTON GAY PRIDE PARADE INVESTIGATED

(Houston) -- An investigation has been launched inside the Houston Police Department over a sergeant's comments as his officers were setting out to patrol this year's Gay Pride Parade in the Montrose area.

An Internal Affairs Division (IAD) complaint has been filed by a Special Operations Division officer, who reports that sergeant repeatedly commented about roughing up and arresting gay people, according to one high-ranking officer who was briefed on the investigation.

The allegations and the IAD investigation were confirmed by a second HPD source, who spoke to a reporter on the condition of anonymity.

"It's a disturbing and frightening comment," said Robert Scamardo, board chair for Equality Texas, a gay rights organization.

The high-ranking officer said the complaint alleges that the Special Operations sergeant was preparing to leave the police station when he was heard uttering comments about roughing up or arresting "fa--ots" before the 2009 Pride Parade.

The complaint was filed near the start of this year's Pride Parade, but the reason for the delay was not clear.

Scamardo says his organization heard of no problems or harassment by police this year, which many saw as progress over the 2009 Pride Parade, when HPD Mounted Patrol officers were accused of harassing spectators and participants.

Plus, Houston had just elected its first openly gay mayor, Annise Parker, who pushed for HPD officers to be allowed to wear their uniforms while marching if they chose. Her policy was first reported on this Examiner page in April.

But that progress is put into perspective by this HPD internal investigation, if you ask Scamardo. He said, "That any police officer with authority would say something like that, especially with supervisory authority to give direction to other police officers ... it's even more frightening and disturbing."

The sergeant remains on duty as the IAD investigation progresses. He will be named here only if the investigation results in a public record such as a reprimand or suspension from duty.

The ranking officer who is familiar with the investigation said the inflammatory comments were made in the presence of a gay officer, but that officer did not file the complaint. A straight officer who heard the remarks ended up filing the formal complaint.

"There's hope and encouragement in that, that everyone doesn't buy into this sort of mentality," Scamardo said of the officer who filed the complaint on his own sergeant. He called that officer stepping forward, "a courageous act."[11]

I agree! That was a truly courageous act. I know from personal experience that reporting a supervisor can wreak havoc on your career. I can only hope that the Houston Police Department will support the officer who made the complaint. This is a great opportunity for the mayor and chief to show the rest of the Houston P.D. what they really expect from their cops. On the other hand, if the complaining officer is left to "twist in the wind," as the Canadian officer put it, the message to the rest of the department will be "NO RATS," and there will be no amount of speechifying that will convince them otherwise.

If the mayor and chief need evidence of what can happen, they need only look due east to Harrison County, Mississippi, where brutality was denied and allowed to continue, in spite of internal complaints.

In February of 2006, two Gulfport, Mississippi, officers brought a drunk and uninjured Jessie Lee Williams to the Harrison County Jail. That night, Williams was beaten to death by Harrison County deputies while he was handcuffed to a restraint chair. Ten deputies were eventually sentenced to prison terms for his death. Deputy

Ryan Teel pled guilty to a life sentence to avoid a trial and possible death sentence.

During the investigation by the Justice Department, deputies admitted they had been beating and abusing prisoners for at least ten years. But it goes back even further than that.

Seventeen years earlier, former Harrison County deputies Tony Lewis and Andrea Gibbs *were fired* after they went public with complaints alleging the abuse of juvenile and adult detainees in the Harrison County jail system. The following excerpts are from a news article on SunHerald.com.

'89 WHISTLE-BLOWERS FEEL VINDICATED
JAILERS WHO ALLEGED ABUSE WERE FIRED
GULFPORT—Former Harrison County jailers fired 17 years ago after going public with allegations of abuse behind bars said they feel vindicated by a recent federal indictment.

Tony Lewis and Andrea Gibbs believe Jessie Lee Williams Jr. would be alive today if authorities had listened to them in 1989. That was the year Lewis, Gibbs and two other deputies were fired after they went public with complaints alleging the abuse of juvenile and adult detainees in the Harrison County jail system . . . .

Fast-forward to March 23, [2007] when Gaston, who most recently ran the jail booking room, and three exjailers were indicted in an alleged conspiracy to deprive inmates of their civil rights.

The federal indictment accuses co-defendant Ryan Teel

of charges involving Williams' fatal beating in February 2006. Gaston is accused of assaulting two inmates in August and October 2005. In related guilty pleas, five ex-jailers have admitted a pattern of abuse existed at the jail for at least five years, according to court documents. Lewis and Gibbs claim the abuse began much earlier. They maintain Gaston and other jail officials in the 1980s encouraged abuse, covered it up and taught officers how to strike inmates with an open palm above the hairline to avoid visible marks . . . .

The indictment is "seventeen years too late," said Lewis, now an ordained minister, "but the Bible says that whatever is done in the dark will be brought to the light. You've got to reap what you sow. It's just a shame that Jessie Williams had to die."

Gibbs said her first day on the job, she saw juvenile-jail warden Homer McKnight Jr. abuse a teenage female inmate. The girl "wouldn't shut up," said Gibbs, who claims McKnight stripped the girl down to her under-wear, cuffed her feet, restrained her hands above her head and shoved the crotch of a dirty uniform in the girl's mouth to silence her.

Lewis said he also witnessed that incident and expressed his concerns with Joe Price, then chief deputy sheriff . . . .

Gibbs said she and Lewis, along with deputies Will Williams and Boyce Grayson Jr., began to document abuse. She said they gathered information on about 75 incidents but weren't prepared to go public until they got an injunction to prevent officials from firing them over their claims.

"Rick Gaston got wind of it," Gibbs said. Gibbs said Gaston took her aside at the jail and told her the four of them should report to the criminal-investigation office in a matter of hours and bring their "evidence." Gibbs said the attorney who accompanied them requested state and federal investigators be present when the documents were turned over. Jail officials refused to make those arrangements, Gibbs said, and the four traveled to the ACLU office in Jackson for a news conference to make their accusations public. The next day the four learned through news reports that they had been fired. "Nobody believed us," said Gibbs. "We thought we were doing the right thing. We thought people would be glad that offi-cers within the jail would stand up for what was right."

Interim District Attorney Joe Meadows presented the allegations to a grand jury, which declined to indict any-one the whistle-blowers accused . . . .

The grand jury review became a witch-hunt against the whistle-blowers, said attorney Wayne Woodall. "They became targets themselves," he said . . . .

Gibbs and Lewis said they were stunned with the grand jury process . . . .

"I don't hold any hard feelings toward any of them now," Lewis said. "But it's a shame the four of us had to go through what we did. It's a shame Jessie Williams had to die . . . ."

Attorney John Whitfield, who represented the four in a

claim accusing the ACLU of failing to represent them in a related lawsuit, calls the four whistle-blowers "heroes."

"They came forward to expose the abuses in the sheriff's department only to have the system, law enforcement, the district attorney's office and the courts, to turn on them," Whitfield said.

"Shame on those political officials who failed to do the right thing. Shame on a system that vilified those who did the right thing. The system protected itself by protecting the wrongdoers. The system failed people like Jessie Lee Williams and many others whose names we may never hear."[12]

This was a system that protected itself, to its own destruction, through the code of silence. In 2007, the author was invited by Chief Alan Weatherford to speak to the Gulfport Police Department about the code of silence. Chief Weatherford required the entire department, cops and civilian employees, to attend. I knew, from my experience, that there is often a close relationship between the sheriff's department and the local police departments. Gulfport, Mississippi, does not have a large department, and when Hurricane Katrina struck, it decimated Gulfport and the surrounding cities. The sheriff's office, local police, state troopers and National Guard troops came to work every day, working without communications or squad cars, in nightmarish conditions. They did this in spite of the fact that many of them lost everything in Katrina and had their own disasters at home. These are brave men and women who showed the world the true meaning of protect and serve! So what happened to Jessie Lee Williams?

I assumed, correctly, that some of the officers in the room were friends and possibly family of those Harrison County deputies. Knowing what they had been through together after Katrina, I told the officers that I could not and would not believe that all the deputies going to prison over Jessie Lee William's death were bad men and women.

So, my question to the group was "If you knew this was going on, why didn't anybody try to stop it?" None of them responded. Many just hung their heads. No rats.

What I didn't know was that the wife of one of the arresting officers was in the audience. She approached me at the break and was very bitter and very angry. She told me the Justice Department had offered her husband a plea agreement of up to seven years in federal prison for not reporting the beating. According to her, her husband did exactly what he was told to do; he kept his mouth shut. As I listened to her words of anger and frustration, I thought about the many times I heard that same message from trainers, peers, supervisors, and on one occasion, a chief.

And I wonder, as you should wonder, how many times has that statement, "Keep your mouth shut," or "No rats" led to officers lying or not reporting what they saw?

If the Houston mayor and chief do not support the officers who come forward with complaints of police misconduct, the message to the rest of the department *will be* "Keep your mouth shut."

But, with or without the support of administrators or

supervisors, we must recognize the damage we do to ourselves and each other every time we allow cops to operate outside the law and hide behind the code. Harrison County, Mississippi, should be a wakeup call to the world about the truly devastating effects of the code of silence.

One department that does not need a wakeup call is the Crystal, Minnesota PD. Several Crystal officers, including a supervisor, testified in Federal Court that Minneapolis Police Officer Jason Andersen's use of force was excessive.

Here are excerpts from the *Minneapolis Star and Tribune* article.

Former Mpls. cop found not guilty of using unreasonable force

A jury took about two hours to decide Jason Andersen did not violate a teen's civil rights. Andersen wants to return to work for Minneapolis police.

A federal jury on Wednesday acquitted former Minneapolis police officer Jason Andersen of charges that he violated a teenager's civil rights by allegedly kicking the boy in the head. . . .

. . . Andersen faced federal charges stemming from an incident during the Crystal Frolics carnival in July 2008. A federal grand jury indicted Andersen for allegedly depriving teenager Jevontay Johnson of his rights by kicking the teen's head while he was on the ground. During the trial, several other police officers testified that Andersen kicked the teen's head.

Andersen, however, denied intentionally doing so. He

said he kicked the boy's shoulder in an effort to make him spread his arms. The jury deliberated only about two hours. After the verdict, Andersen bear-hugged his attorney, then embraced several friends in the hallway outside the Minneapolis courtroom.[13]

I commend Officer Jerry Krob and the other Crystal Police Officers for their willingness to stand up for what's right. Crystal Police Chief John Banick stood by his officers throughout this case and he stands as an example of what a Chief should be to his officers.

I don't know Jason Anderson. I know he has gone through some real ordeals in the last few years. In this case, Andersen was made to stand trial for his conduct and he was found not-guilty. Going through a trial like this is not easy. I know I've been there. If Jason Andersen sees this as a wakeup call he is likely to have a successful career. Moreover, like it or not, he will owe that success to the Crystal officers who put their reputations on the line to tell the truth about what they witnessed.

I hope for his sake that he can make it happen.

We can change the police culture from within. Policing ourselves should mean that we don't allow the misconduct in the first place.

A friend of mine related the following story. He was new to the narcotics unit, and on his first night with the team they told him he would be driving. They picked up a street dealer and, as they drove away with him in the back seat, the narcotics cops started punching their non-prisoner. My friend is a really big man. He reached into the back seat and literally dragged the drug dealer into the front seat with him. He told the cops in the back seat "Not here. Not now. I don't work like that." They stopped. He let the shaken street dealer go. The "team" he had just joined did what they could to show their displeasure with my friend's high integrity, but as long as he was around they stopped their criminal behavior. One cop can make a difference.

I still get asked for advice about the same issues I experienced twenty years ago. In February 2003, a young officer's mother told me that her son, a graduate of one of my academies four years earlier, was thinking about quitting because of the illegal and unethical behavior he was seeing at the precinct where he works.

Recently, I talked to a new officer assigned to one of our first ring suburbs. This is an agency with a great reputation and, in my opinion, an outstanding chief. The new officer was unprepared for the "congratulations" he got from his training officer and other senior officers when he opted not to cite an off-duty cop caught in a speed trap. He told me it wasn't that he thought it was a big deal. The off-duty cop was going only seven miles an hour over the limit. He said he wouldn't tag anyone for seven over. What bothered him was that the other cops were so supportive of the idea that we are immune from the law. Now his question to me is, "When are we not immune?" "Is there a limit?" "How will I know?" "Where's the line?"

His frustration with what to do about a cop traffic violator is understandable. I worked with a supervisor who consistently, and deliberately, ran late for appointments. She thought nothing of driving 90 miles an hour to get to the next meeting. A young peace officer who previously worked directly for this same supervisor was assigned to work for me. In my first experience riding with her in an unmarked vehicle, we were going to lunch when she started running red lights. When I told her to stop she became very angry. Her comment to me was, "Who's going to stop me?"

This idea that we are immune from traffic citations is a direct result of the corrupting influence of the Code. Our discretionary power is immense and we are not required to cite every speeder who comes down the road, and we don't. But we have sworn to "protect and serve," and I don't remember anything in the police code of ethics that talked about immunity under the law as part of protecting and serving.

Here's a perfect example from the *Minneapolis StarTribune*, March 2, 2004.

> A state trooper has been disciplined for his role in a high-speed ride in a colleague's patrol car that hit another car while taking him to play in a hockey game in Eagan. Trooper Mike Olson has been suspended without pay for 30 days, said State Patrol spokesman Kevin Smith. Olson is expected to appeal the decision, Smith said. Olson got a flat tire the night of Dec. 18 as he was about to leave his Lino Lakes home to play on a State Patrol hockey team. Trooper Jennifer Schneider was on duty and heard

he needed a ride. She picked him up and drove down Interstate Hwy. 35E to Eagan at speeds exceeding 110 miles per hour with lights and sirens on. She also had a State Patrol-sponsored Explorer Scout riding with her that night. Schneider hit a car that was trying to get out of her way in Eagan; she told local police it happened while she was chasing a traffic offender. Nobody was hurt, and an officer took Olson to the game before another trooper arrived. Schneider told him that her only passenger was the scout. An anonymous tip led to an investigation. Schneider was charged with gross-misdemeanor misconduct. She has resigned.

NO COP IS ALL GOOD OR ALL BAD

I don't expect cops to be perfect. No matter what we do we are still human, and no cop is all good or all bad. Cops, for the most part, are the greatest people in the world and are capable of heroic acts. And most cops, surprisingly, will never ask for, nor are they given, any special recognition for their daily acts of heroism. Instead, you might see a line in a report that says, "I reached into the front seat of the vehicle and after disengaging the seatbelt removed the victim."

What often goes unsaid and unreported are the flames coming up from under the car. The smoke that made it impossible to see what was happening. The screaming for help coming from another passenger in the car. The blood-soaked uniform. The hours at the hospital while they bandage the burns on the cop's arms and hands. The phone call a partner had to make to the spouse or loved one (if they didn't already see it on television), and the second guessing that cop will do for the rest of their life about not saving the other passenger, the child's mother. Violent death becomes an intimate part of every cop's life, and we record on paper and deep in our souls the details, horror, and despair. We try to make sense of senseless acts—for the sake of the victims and ourselves.

We will be the only ones there to hear the last breath of someone's spouse, child or parent; and we will remember and live with that. Far too often, when we are too late to help, we are the first person a family turns to for an explanation of why their loved one had to die. And when all else fails, we will take lives and live with that burden.

FRIENDLY FIRE

February 25, 2003, a Minneapolis Police officer mistakenly shot multiple times an undercover Minneapolis Police Officer, who had already been shot by a suspect who had escaped. The officer doing the shooting was responding to the injured officer's call for help. It doesn't get any worse than that. The cops who are spared that kind of horrendous experience all know it could just as easily be them in the future. Yet, we go to work every day and face that risk and others just as great. Statistically we can show that policing is a relatively safe job, but it is one of the few jobs, outside of the president and the Armed Forces, where you know people will deliberately try to kill you.

I know cops who could be described as racist and brutal but are the most compassionate and tender-hearted people you can imagine around children of all races. And, can there be any greater example of police bravery and commitment to the public we serve than the demonstrated acts of heroism on 9/11? No one had to ask if these cops would go into the towers—we all knew they would.

We will never be completely free of the Code of Silence. It is as much a part of policing as illness is a part of living. It is a necessary infection of our spirit that makes us more resistant to future corruption—when we choose to see it for what it really is. But this is a choice each of us must make on our own. No one else will make it for us, and the Code will fight back. The choice of being a "peace officer" means there will be many battles in solitary combat with other cops and with yourself. You will not win them all—you cannot, the cards are stacked against you. There will be no medals, awards ceremonies, or cheering crowds for the battles you do win. But there will be honor and integrity—in your life and in your work.

> The last of the human freedoms, to choose one's attitude
> in any given set of circumstances, to choose one's own
> way. (Viktor E. Frankl, 1905–1997)

And Then There Is the Law

The Fourth Amendment of the U.S. Constitution is a simple statement of the rights of any and all persons who live in the United States, its territories and the District of Columbia. It is the guiding amendment for law enforcement at all levels. When we violate the provisions of the 4th Amendment we can be held liable. All too often it is the code of silence that leads us down that path. Read the following articles carefully and note what caused the demise of the officers involved.

A peace officer can act within department policy, act within state law, and still go to prison for violation of a person's civil rights. Under both Title 42 U.S. Code Section 1983 (§1983) and Title 18 U.S. Code Section 242 (§242), peace officers and those helping them or working with them can be held liable for both civil (§1983) and criminal (§242) damages. Following is the law as it applies to those who operate under the color of law and afterward I have included just a few examples. Again, it is not just your ethics, it is the ethics of all those who work with you and for you. Protect yourself first, but always protect your brother or sister peace officer too.

Sec. 1983.

42 U.S. Code Section 1983—Civil action for deprivation of rights

STATUTE

Every person who, under color of any statute, ordinance, regulation, custom, or usage, of any State or Territory or the District of Columbia, subjects, or causes to be subjected, any citizen of the United States or other person within the jurisdiction thereof to the deprivation of any rights, privileges, or immunities secured by the Constitution and laws, shall be liable to the party injured in an action at law, suit in equity, or other proper proceeding for redress, except that in any action brought against a judicial officer for an act or omission taken in such officer's judicial capacity, injunctive relief shall not be granted unless a declaratory decree was violated or declaratory relief was unavailable. For the purposes of this section, any Act of Congress applicable exclusively to the District of Columbia shall be considered to be a statute of the District of Columbia.[14]

18 U.S. Code Sec. 242. Deprivation of rights under color of law

STATUTE

Whoever, under color of any law, statute, ordinance, regulation, or custom, willfully subjects any person in any State, Territory, Commonwealth, Possession, or District to the deprivation of any rights, privileges, or immunities secured or protected by the Constitution or laws of the United States, or to different punishments, pains, or penalties, on account of such person being an alien, or by reason of his color, or race, than are prescribed for the punishment of citizens, shall be fined under this title or imprisoned not more than one year, or both; and if bodily injury results from the acts committed in violation of this section or if such acts include the use, attempted use, or threatened use of a dangerous weapon, explosives, or fire, shall be fined under this title or imprisoned not more than ten years, or both; and if death results from the acts committed in violation of this section or if such acts include kidnapping or an attempt to kidnap, aggravated sexual abuse, or an attempt to commit aggravated sexual abuse, or an attempt to kill, shall be fined under this title, or imprisoned for any term of years or for life, or both, or may be sentenced to death.[15]

THREE FORMER ATLANTA POLICE OFFICERS
SENTENCED TO FEDERAL PRISON IN FATAL
SHOOTING OF ELDERLY ATLANTA WOMAN.
DEFENDANTS PLEADED GUILTY TO CONSPIRACY
TO VIOLATE CIVIL RIGHTS RESULTING IN THE
DEATH OF 92-YEAR OLD ATLANTA RESIDENT
KATHRYN JOHNSTON.

In a brief news conference after the sentencing hearings,
United States Attorney David E. Nahmias said in part,
"As Atlanta police narcotics officers, these three defendants repeatedly failed to follow proper procedures and
then lied under oath to obtain search warrants. Their routine violations of the Fourth Amendment led to the death
of an innocent citizen. The death of Kathryn Johnston in
a police shooting was a terrible tragedy for a law-abiding
elderly woman, her family, and friends and our entire
community. But as her family and others hoped, from
this tragedy have come two positive results. First, it has
led the Atlanta Police Department to implement useful reforms in training and supervision and to entirely
revamp its Narcotics Unit, reducing the possibility of
a similar tragedy in the future. Second, the significant
prison sentences imposed by the Court today should
send a strong message to other law enforcement officers
who may be tempted to lie under oath or otherwise violate the law. Officers who think, as these defendants once
did, that the ends justify the means or that 'taking short-
cuts' and telling lies will not be discovered and punished
should realize that they are risking their careers and their

liberty. And officers who try to obstruct justice when their misconduct faces exposure, rather than cooperating in the investigation, should realize that they will face even more severe punishment."[16]

TWO FORMER BIRMINGHAM POLICE OFFICERS INDICTED FOR CIVIL RIGHTS VIOLATIONS.

BIRMINGHAM—A federal grand jury today indicted two former members of the Birmingham Police Department for using unreasonable force during a January 2008 arrest, the U.S. Department of Justice announced in conjunction with U.S. Attorney Joyce White Vance.

The one-count indictment filed in U.S. District Court charges that BARRETT GENE DEWITT and DAVID WAYNE DORAN, while acting in their official capacity as police officers, aided and abetted one another in striking the individual they were arresting with fists, feet, and a baton on Jan. 23, 2008. Those blows caused bodily injury to the individual, who is identified in the indictment as A.W.

"Most law enforcement officers work every day to protect us and they earn our confidence by performing their duties with honor and integrity," Vance said. "Police officers who use unreasonable force must be brought to account so that we can all feel safe and have trust in the officers who are there to protect us."

According to the indictment, DEWITT and DORAN violated the victim's civil rights by depriving A.W. of his Fourth Amendment constitutional right to be free of unreasonable seizures, which includes the right to be free from the use of unreasonable force by someone acting under the color of law.[17]

THREE FORMER MILWAUKEE POLICE OFFICERS SENTENCED ON CIVIL RIGHTS-RELATED CHARGES

WASHINGTON—Former Milwaukee, Wis., police officers Jon Bartlett, Andrew Spengler, and Daniel Masarik were sentenced today in federal court on civil rights charges arising out of the October 2004 assault of Frank Jude and Lovell Harris by off-duty Milwaukee police officers. Bartlett was sentenced to 208 months imprisonment; Spengler was sentenced to 188 months imprisonment; and Masarik was sentenced to 188 months imprisonment. After release from prison, each will be on federal supervised release for three years.On July 26, 2007, a federal jury in Milwaukee found Bartlett, Spengler and Masarik guilty of conspiring to violate the civil rights of Jude and Harris, and of violating the civil rights of Jude. Previously in April 2006, all three were acquitted of state charges related to the assault on Jude and Harris.[18]

NATCHEZ, MISSISSIPPI POLICE OFFICERS INDICTED FOR CIVIL RIGHTS OFFENSES, CONSPIRACY TO COMMIT IDENTITY THEFT AND FRAUD, AND FALSE STATEMENTS

Elvis Prater was charged with two counts of deprivation of rights under color of law and one count of false statements. If convicted, he faces a maximum punishment of 10 years in prison for the civil rights offenses and five years in prison for the false statements offense. Dewayne

Johnson was charged with two counts of deprivation of rights under color of law, one count of conspiracy to commit identity theft, credit card fraud, and bank fraud, and two counts of false statements. If convicted, he faces a maximum punishment of 10 years in prison for the civil rights offenses and five years in prison for the conspiracy and false statements offenses.

According to the indictment, on May 23, 2009, Elvis Prater assaulted two arrestees who were in custody of the Natchez Police Department, Dewayne Johnson failed to protect an arrestee in his patrol car from Prater's assault, and Johnson stole credit and debit cards from an arrestee in his custody.[19]

I included this last case against the Natchez, Mississippi police officers because it is important to note that the charges included: "Dewayne Johnson failed to protect an arrestee in his patrol car."

How many times have officers been a party to the failure to protect a person in custody and not reported it? Most of those abuses are small, in terms of the injuries or damage done, but they are still abuses and most officers, most of the time, will avoid prosecution because of the code of silence. Police officers have a difficult job. Decisions we make in a split second can be reviewed over a period of years before the courts come to a final decision on whether our actions were justified. It behooves all of us to prepare for those split-second decisions.

What we *do* to prepare ourselves in terms of officer survival is critical to our both our career and personal survival. Being ethical is not just about what we do for ourselves. We will all make mistakes. We will all lose our temper. We will all be tempted to cross the line and put ourselves and other officers at risk. It is no longer enough that we are individually ethical. We must also hold each other accountable, or the courts will.

How will you explain to your partner's wife and children why you didn't intervene when it was clear that what they were doing was wrong? Will you wait 'till your partner goes to prison to say, "I should have stopped them," or will you have the courage to say: "Not here. Not now. Not in front of me!"

Newspaper Columns

IN FEBRUARY OF 2007, I started writing a monthly column on police ethics for Officer.com. It was an interesting experience. The following chapter is a collection of some those columns, in no particular order. Maybe you will see yourself in some of them and you will find some comfort in my words, as some veteran officers have. If you are new to policing maybe you will find some words of forewarning; not that it will prevent you from making a mistake. If you put on that uniform you will occasionally make bad choices. The irony is that you will probably make those choices for what seems like the right reason.

I can't tell you how to do this job. All I can say is that when things go badly try to figure out what went wrong and fix it so it doesn't happen again. And remember, no battle ever goes according to plan. The important part is that you engage in that battle. Doing nothing will only lead to disaster.

You have sworn to put your life on the line for your fellow officers in their times of greatest need, and I know you will if it comes to that. Now bring up that same courage and put yourself on the line today by promising that when you see your brother or sister officer, agent, deputy, or guard doing something that could cost them their career, their family, or maybe their life, you will say:

I'M NOT GOING TO LET YOU DO THAT.

NOT HERE! NOT NOW! NOT IN FRONT OF ME!

MORAL BODY ARMOR
WEAVING OUR OWN PROTECTION,
ONE THREAD AT A TIME.

I hate it when I'm asked to follow my own advice about ethics! It's easy, in retrospect, to talk about some of the tough ethical choices I made during my career. And I know I have minimized a lot of the bad choices I made in favor of a more acceptable memory; so be it. Still, there are plenty that bother me to this day. There was the young Native American burglar who was also stealing cars. I really showed him how tough I was, punching him while he was in handcuffs, thinking I was going to get some sort of useful information from him. The only one who was tough was him. He never said a word.

He taught me something that night. He taught me that I was weak because I didn't have the guts to <u>not</u> punch him after my training officer told me to. I'm sure I taught that young man something too, that cops are brutal and stupid. There is probably no way that kid will ever change his attitude about cops after what I did that night. His family probably feels the same way. There was one change that took place that night, in me. I swore I would never do something like that again. I felt terrible. I made plenty of other mistakes in later years but punching someone in handcuffs just to hurt them was not one of them. Almost thirty years later, as I sat down to write a book on police ethics I thought about that incident and I wanted to write something that would help new officers make better choices than I made.

So I wrote about the importance of stepping in and stopping another officer when their conduct gets out of line. It makes a lot more sense to me than going to internal affairs or civilian review with relatively minor offenses. But I had forgotten how hard it can be to take that step, till recently.

I was working with this person for the first time. They seemed full of energy and ready and willing to take on the world but they were treating prisoners like shit and clearly making them angry. It was a small thing really. The prisoners were hardcore gang members. They'd been through the system before and it was no surprise to them that the cellblock was cold. They knew before we closed the door that blankets were available so they asked for them, respectfully, if not politely. My partner's response was "Does this look like the fucking Marriott Hotel to you?" Then my partner walked them into their cell without the blankets. His response to their request for blankets surprised me but not as much as my own reluctance to say something to him right then and there. I wasn't going to say anything in front of the prisoners, but here was a situation exactly as I outlined in my book, a minor incident with a chance to step in and make a small difference and yet I hesitated.

Don't get me wrong. I am not in the business of making life

comfortable for gang members that are on their way to their next prison cell. But making prisoners angry just because you can is an officer safety issue. I didn't want them acting out their anger on me or someone else just because my partner felt it was necessary to demonstrate that he was in control. A minute or two later I got the blankets out and was walking them back to the prisoners when my partner started chipping on me about being nice to criminals. I responded by reminding him that they were more likely to nap or at least lay down and relax if they had a blanket to keep warm. His response was unpleasant.

A couple days later I am in the courtroom with the same partner and once again he is going out of his way to make a prisoner unhappy. By now I have had a couple days to think about what I should have said to him the first time we worked together and I go through a short litany of why making a prisoner angry, just for the sake of making him angry, potentially compromises another officer's safety. His response was ambiguous at best but I think I might have reached him on some level. At the very least he knows what to expect from me.

But the question I had to ask myself was, "Why wasn't I able to challenge him immediately when the bad behavior first occurred?" That's what I advocate when I speak about moral courage yet, when it came time, I hesitated. I was reminded that it's hard to step in like that, even on relatively minor issues. Maybe that's the problem. On big, clear-cut, in your face, go-to-jail-lose-your-job issues the decision to step in is almost made for you. It's the smaller ones that we feel safe walking away from. We can rationalize that they are no big deal because no one is getting hurt and it's just a whole lot easier if we don't confront our coworkers.

But we don't develop moral courage from walking away. Like the body armor you wear with your uniform your moral body armor is made up of many very small threads, woven in a special pattern, a pattern that you weave and create each and every time you take on one of the small issues. And likewise, every time you walk away a thread goes missing from the pattern and you are the weaker for it. Doing the right thing is hard and it can be especially hard with the smaller issues because they are the easiest to walk away from. Think about the pattern you are weaving with your life.

Weave a pattern that matters.

WHO KILLS THE MOST COPS?

Hugh Thompson, Jr., died January 6, 2006, at the age of 62. Thompson wasn't a cop and that name won't mean much to younger cops. He didn't die in a gun battle. He died of cancer. But it's not Thompson's death that's important; it's what he did with his life. On March 16, 1968, Warrant Officer Hugh Thompson was a helicopter pilot in the Viet Nam war and was flying cover over the village of My Lai when he witnessed American soldiers killing unarmed men, women and children.

Hugh Thompson flew his helicopter into the middle of the slaughter that was occurring and had his gunners point their guns at our own soldiers in order to protect a group of 10 non-combatants hiding in a bunker. He saved their lives, evacuating men, women, and children that would have been killed if not for his intervention. Up to 200 other men, women and children in My Lai were not so lucky.

How many of us would have had the courage to do what Hugh Thompson did? How many times have you witnessed acts of brutality and stepped in to stop it? Or did you just go along to get along and keep to the code of silence? I ask that because most of the soldiers at My Lai didn't step up to report what happened and I have to believe that most of those soldiers were not bad men. In fact many of the men refused to participate in the slaughter. But they didn't stop the others. Only Thompson had the guts.

The fact that men are capable of extreme acts of violence is no surprise. We witness first hand what people are capable of doing to each other. The news stories of children raped and murdered, or body parts strewn around the scene of an accident caused by a drunk driver are not "news" to us, they are part of our daily life. And as the sheep dogs of society we understand the value and necessity of our own capacity for violence toward those human predators.

But what do you do when the violence being committed by one of your own becomes abuse? How many times have you walked away with the comment "I want no part of this" when what you should have done was step in and stop the violence? Hugh Thompson risked his life, and the life of his crewmen, to protect people he couldn't really be sure weren't the enemy. Cops are supposed to protect each other. You wouldn't let another officer walk into an ambush. Why do you walk away when they've lost control and they really need your help?

We spend a lot of time and money on officer survival training and we talk about how important it is to stick together and protect each other; but what are we doing to save the lives and careers of cops who are engaged in unethical or illegal conduct? The National P.O.L.I.C.E. Suicide Foundation estimates that there are at least 300 suicides each year in law enforcement. The reported number is only about a third of that, but if you've been in uniform for a while you've seen the "accidents" that never got reported as suicide.

USA Today reported in 1997: "One of the common factors in suicide by law enforcement officers: an officer under investigation. One of the common police suicide warning signs: a rise in citizen complaints about aggressiveness. There is no particular profile of the officer who will attempt suicide. He or she may be a few years out of the academy or at the end of their career, and their personal crises run the gamut. Divorce and the break-up of relationships are common problems. But those who kill themselves may also be suffering from stagnated careers, *under investigation for alleged misconduct* or drinking heavily. Throw the ever-present firearm into the cauldron and the mix is deadly." © 1997 *USA Today*

Most cops work very hard to do the job the way it is supposed to be done, but none of us are perfect. We all have bad days and we are all capable of violence toward people who probably don't deserve it. We should be able to depend on each other when our own judgment goes awry. A real partner wouldn't let you do something stupid that threatens your career, or your life. And how many lives and careers could we save if we just stepped in at those critical times and said "Not Here, Not Now."

In 1975 there were only a few of us that wore body armor. It was uncomfortable and we caught hell from the old timers who told us body armor wouldn't save anybody. They were right in part; body armor doesn't save everybody, but it saves some, and it would still be worth it if it only saved one life. An attitude of "Not Here and Not Now" won't make a difference to some officers, but it will be worth it if it saves just one life.

To prevent suicides, Robert Douglas, executive director of the National P.O.L.I.C.E. Suicide Foundation and a retired Baltimore police officer says: "Officers must be taught what signs to look for and encouraged to talk to co-workers who might need help. In his book, *Death with No Valor, & Hope Beyond The Badge,* Douglas recounts the story of an officer who took an unloaded gun, put it in his mouth and pulled the trigger to see if he could. Then the officer loaded the weapon and was about to shoot himself when his cat walked into the room. "He stroked that cat and said 'who will take care of this stinking cat if I kill myself,'" Douglas wrote. "And that was enough to stop him. How hard is it to save an officer if his cat could do it?" © 1997 *USA Today*

Check out The National P.O.L.I.C.E. Suicide Foundation http:// www.psf.org/index.htm

NOBODY CARES ABOUT A FREE CUP OF COFFEE!

Police ethics training is finally coming into its own. It is being offered for in-service, pre-service, and in college law enforcement programs. Unfortunately, we still seem to be a little short, in some cases, on a curriculum that successfully blends the history of moral thought and ethics with current police issues. I recently talked to an officer that has gone back to school to finish his 4 year degree in criminal justice. He is a successful police sergeant, raised in a poorer section of the city, in circumstances that sent many of his one-time friends into criminal careers. He is a success story because of the choices he made in his life. He did not do it alone and he gives credit where credit is due, but in the end he made the choices that led to his success.

I was talking to him about a recent class he took in police ethics and his only comment was "What a bunch of shit!" He went on to explain that he thought the professor was an academic without a clue about the real problems cops, and people, face on the job and in their lives. I know the professor he talked about. He is a very well educated man who could spend all day debating "What would Socrates do?" based on his knowledge of the great moral thinkers. He could tell you why a free cup of coffee is the beginning of the end; a slippery slope that leads to moral depravity. And he has no experience in policing so for all his knowledge he couldn't connect with my friend, too bad.

Last week a student in my Domestic Violence class volunteered that she just finished the worst class in her college experience, Police

Ethics 101. This student has opinions about everything and it was interesting that her reasons for disliking the class were similar to my friend's reasons; there was nothing about the real dilemmas people face. It was all about the history of ethics and the proverbial free cup of coffee, combined with matching names to moral theories.

There are good ethics teachers out there. I heard one ethics teacher comment that he was there to "teach what others have thought about right and wrong behavior." He didn't claim to be an ethicist or a philosopher. He saw himself as a facilitator; someone who would walk you through what others said or wrote about ethics and help you apply it to your circumstances, to real life. He also believed that he was there to learn from others about what works and what doesn't. I am not talking about situational ethics where we can apply the ethics that best benefit our purpose. That's the purview of politicians, and I don't do well with politicians.

I would guess that at this point every police department in the United States has an official policy against taking a free cup of coffee. My question is this: How many of you abide by that policy? I never did. If they didn't charge me for the coffee I left a tip big enough to cover the difference. If they wouldn't charge me for a meal I left a tip big enough to cover that too. I didn't get up and say "Sorry madam I can't take free food." There is no moral dilemma in free food. Pay for it; it is that simple. It only becomes a dilemma when you see your sergeant or maybe even your chief taking gratuities that you know she has told you not to take. Who do you report that to?

If you really want to teach ethics to cops or law enforcement students, then talk about the real problems cops face. Like what do you do when your partner lies in his police report or loses control and really hurts someone. Most ethics classes will tell you that it is a simple decision, you turn them in. Really? What about the time that partner saved your life? Or the time that same partner put her own life on the line to save a citizen's life? Are going to run to IA and turn them in. I don't think so. It would take a pretty depraved or criminal act for most cops to step up and report to internal affairs or civilian review and in those cases they should. I'm not saying you shouldn't do something about the smaller things, I am saying you should be prepared from ethics training to make the right decision about what to do, whether it's stepping in and stopping the behavior or taking it to the boss or IA. For the most part I don't think we do a very good job of that.

I have talked to cops from several jurisdictions across the U.S. about the issues I wrote about in *Walking With the Devil*. I asked them if their ethics training addressed any of those issues and the answer was almost always "Hell No!" One young officer who asked that I not use his name told me that when he read my book it was as if "You were looking over my shoulder at what was happening to me for the first two weeks on the job." I asked him if he had been prepared for that in any of his training and he said "No."

As I was growing up I learned a very important lesson; you can't win the game if you don't know the rules. Ethics class is a great opportunity to teach new officers the rules. Talk about ethics in terms of what bad decisions can mean to officer safety, to career survival, and to emotional survival. Show them that there are viable options to some of the unethical behavior they will witness or be asked to participate in. Be honest. There is a lot of discussion that will go on in any class about the options available when you are faced with a real dilemma and those are the kind of discussions you should be having in police ethics classes. Nobody cares about a free coffee. They care about their career, their partners, their family, and their life, and ethics classes should be a chance to talk honestly about real life.

WILL YOU SLEEP WITH ME FOR A MILLION DOLLARS? HOW ABOUT ONE DOLLAR?

A student asked me the following question the other day. "Isn't it true," she started, sounding like a lawyer, "That when you covered for cops that committed minor offenses or broke some rule of conduct, that you promoted the code of silence as their supervisor?" I had to admit that it could be seen that way. I went on to explain that I didn't let the conduct slide, I just dealt with the officer on a one to one basis and made it clear that I didn't expect to see the conduct repeated. As a supervisor that was usually enough to get their attention, and no I didn't take every violation or improper use of force to IA. Although I had to admit that there were times when I thought that a two by four between the eyes would have been a lot more effective than my comments. She wasn't satisfied with my answer and pressed on by saying that she thought I was as guilty as the officer committing the offense if I didn't report the conduct to Internal Affairs or Civilian Review for discipline, as required by the police manual.

This was a smart but very young woman and even though I thought her comment was insightful, it showed a lack of life experience. I didn't have all night to explain the different theories on first line supervision or police discretion, so I took another tack. I told her that all cops buy into the code of silence at one time or another and that the important thing is that they understand what it is they are doing to themselves. There are times in every cop's career when they will protect their partner or friend and if they do it knowing the consequences and if they are willing to live with that then there is nothing I am going to say or do to change their mind.

She came back with the comment that it sounded to her like I, meaning me, talked a good game of ethics but that it didn't sound like I was willing to really be ethical. I thought about the price I'd paid for not reporting everything I witnessed and the even bigger price I had paid in terms of friendships for trying to promote good ethics. I was reminded at that point about a Rodney Dangerfield joke I'd heard a long time ago.

A man approaches a beautiful woman in a bar and without any small talk asks her "If I give you a dollar will you sleep with me?" The woman is instantly angry and tells the man "Absolutely not!" Before she can get away from the man he asks her a second question. "Will you sleep with me for a million dollars?" Now the woman pauses and after some thought says "Yes, I will."

The man responds, "How about for twenty dollars?" Again the woman looks indignant and says, "Of course not. What kind of a woman do you think I am?" The man replies, "I thought we just settled that. I was just negotiating the price." Ba Da Boom!

It's a funny joke but there is a lot of truth in there. Most of us have a price; there will always be a code of silence; and cops will always find some justification for using it to protect another cop or themselves. But the fact that they are willing to pay the price doesn't make it right. The code of silence is sort of like smoking. With all the available information out there about the damage smoking does to the smoker, to the fetus in pregnant women, and to those who are forced to inhale second-hand smoke there is no reason why anyone should smoke, but they do.

They can deny the damage all they want and they can come up with some very creative and justifiable reasons for why they do it. That doesn't change the act and it doesn't make it right. If you do it for a million dollars, for twenty dollars, or just because you can, you still do it. The only question is "What are you willing to give up for your act?" That is the real bottom line.

Over the years I heard many cops say "I will never turn in my partners" or "I will stick by them no matter what." But they don't. Not when their own life is going down the tubes. What are you going to do when it's your family that you are sacrificing? Are you really willing to cover for another cop when the results could be the loss of your job or going to prison and losing your family? Where will your partners be then? Do you think your partners will be there volunteering to do your prison time or pay your mortgage while you are gone? Loyalty bought with the code of silence is quickly traded for a few less years or maybe even a chance to lead a life after police work, if that kind of deal is offered.

As a supervisor or a partner you are obligated to protect other officers and sometimes that means protecting them from themselves. Not everything should go to IA. I've pulled a partner off a suspect when my partner was getting out of control and I've been pulled off of suspects when I was losing it. We didn't run to IA but we talked about it. My best partners, and best supervisors, would stop me when I was doing something stupid so they didn't have to cover for me, or report me to IA.

I mentioned earlier that there is also a price to pay for being ethical and it can be a high price. The difference is that you get something worthwhile for the price: Honor and Self Respect. My final question to you is "Are you willing to tell your partner's wife and kids that you could have stopped him and saved his career, and kept him from going to prison, but you chose not to?" Think about it.

IT'S GETTING BETTER ALL THE TIME,
BETTER, BETTER, BEEETTER . . . .

My apologies to the Beetles for using a line from their song, but I just read the latest statistics from Dr. Neal Trautman's research into police attitudes about misconduct and there is much to be excited about. Only 10 years ago research showed that 60% of the cops interviewed would not be inclined to turn in another cop for serious misconduct. As of 2007 the latest research shows that number has dropped to 46%. Even if we factor in statistical error and the fact that the questions were not exactly the same, it still looks to me like cops are demanding more of their fellow officers, and that's good news for all of us.

I just finished doing four days of "ethics training" about the code of silence for the cops of Gulfport, Mississippi. They impressed me with their questions, with their comments, and their honesty about what's right and what's wrong with policing. I was always under the impression, being a white liberal Yankee, that racism played a big part in the day to day lives of cops in the south. My conversations with black and white officers alike left me with the feeling that there may be more racism in the north than there is down on the gulf coast. I also walked away from that department thinking "What a great bunch of cops!" I know they aren't all perfect, but Chief Weatherford has a good department and I wonder if the citizens of Gulfport really know how good their department is? Unfortunately, they may be under the mistaken impression that all cops in Mississippi are brutal. There is a reason for that.

If you've been halfway awake for the last couple years you are aware that a number of Harrison County, Mississippi, deputies are going to federal prison following the beating death of a prisoner that was brought in by the Gulfport Police. The incident brought to light the fact that the use of excessive force had been a common occurrence in the jail for some time. I brought up the Harrison

County case to the Gulfport P.D. this week. I told them that I don't for one minute believe that all those deputies were bad people. I also told them that I don't believe that they got into police work just to beat up people; so what went wrong there? Why didn't someone stop it before it was too late?

I don't know why men and women cross the moral line and start believing that it's OK to hurt people just because they can. In the book *Ordinary Men* the author talks about German businessmen and shopkeepers that were drafted into Hitler's police corps and then assigned to kill Jews. Some of them could not and would not do it, but many did kill, willingly. These were not men who volunteered because they wanted to go out and kill people. There was nothing in their background that would have identified them as killers, yet, when they believed that it was within the law and when they were ordered to murder innocent men, women, and children, they did. I think we have to assume, based on the history of the "final solution" in Germany and the admitted years of brutality in the Harrison County case that there is the potential for murder, or at least brutality, in a lot of us, if not all of us. We have the law to stop us, but the law isn't riding next to us in the squad or helping us fight off a maniacal meth addict on a traffic stop. But very often there is someone there, your backup or your partner.

You put our lives on the line every day for other cops without question and I know that the Gulf Coast law enforcement community worked to save lives putting themselves at great risk in unimaginable conditions. I heard a great comparison made between 9/11 and Hurricane Katrina: after 9/11 you could go home at night to your home and family, there was no such "safe harbor" for the officers responding to Katrina. Many of them lost everything they had and some are just now getting back into their own homes. One of the most impressive things I've ever heard about cops was Chief Weatherford's analysis of his department's response to the disaster: He told me, to paraphrase, that they all stayed and did their jobs till it was done in conditions resembling a third world country in the middle of a war zone.

I told them in Gulfport, and I'll say it again here, you made us all proud to be cops and first responders. And yet, in the case of Harrison County they couldn't, or wouldn't step up and say "That's a bad idea," or "Don't do that" when it was clear that it was wrong. Why is that so hard? It doesn't seem like it should be, yet it is. I talked to a former Iraq war veteran who is also a veteran police officer and even he thinks it's hard to tell another cop to stop something that is easily recognizable as unethical or even criminal conduct.

46% of cops still might not report serious misconduct by other police officers. Almost 10,000 officers have been decertified by the 26 agencies that report those officers. With a little bit of extrapolation that's about 2.5% of the total number of sworn law enforcement in the U.S. That's good, but it could be better. You want to make sure your partner goes home at night? When you see them crossing the line you owe it to them and their families to step in and say: "Not here, not now, not in front of me."

The whole world was watching after Katrina. Gulfport Mississippi PD, you made us proud!

IT'S OK HE'S A FRIEND OF MINE
MARTY RAFFERTY: WHAT BEING A FRIEND SHOULD REALLY MEAN

I worked with Marty Rafferty for a couple years when he was a manager in the personnel division of the Minneapolis Police Department. We kept in touch, exchanging Emails, getting together a couple times over the last few years. When somebody brought up his name I always said "I know Marty, he's a good friend." People assume that when you say "good friend" that you are talking about someone you see fairly often. As you get older you realize that isn't always the case, and it certainly wasn't the case with me and Marty.

Marty died recently. He was only 54 years old. Overweight and a smoker, Marty left a wonderful wife and family behind. It was a sad reviewal and I'll miss him.

Marty's death made me think a lot about what being a friend really means. He was the kind of friend who had a way of helping you out, even when you didn't know you needed help. He would call me up to have lunch at some small out of the way sandwich shop where we could talk, away from city hall. Then as he made small talk he would gently bring up the issue that he wanted to talk about. I must admit that at times it took me a while to figure out where he was going with a particular conversation. Sometimes he took several lunches or coffee meetings to get to a particular point, but he always got there. And he got there in a manner that made it clear he wanted what was in my best interest, not his. Marty really wanted the best for people that worked for him.

In the "blue" world I had a lot of cops tell me they were my friends. In many cases this meant that they expected me to be their friend in return. Friend being another word for that code of silence relationship; cover for me because I'll cover for you. More than once I got into investigations or operations with some of these so called friends only to find out too late what their friendship required. During a routine traffic stop many years ago my partner and I stopped a young woman for speeding. Not a big deal really, 15 over in a 30 zone. But what happened next became a big deal. While I was asking her about her current residence, etc, she interjected that officer so-and-so, a cop on our shift, was a friend of hers. I told her "That's nice" and walked back to the squad with her license, intending to write her for the violation. When I told my partner what she said he told me I should just let her go. In fact he was very emphatic about it. I was still fairly new as a cop and even though it burned me to do it, I let her go with a verbal warning.

It wasn't like I tagged everyone for every traffic violation; it was the idea that someone claiming to be a "friend" meant I should compromise myself. It happened many times over the years as I learned that being a "friend" of certain politicians meant a free ride, charges dropped, arresting officers criticized for not following the rules about "friends." In the end I learned that real friends never ask you to compromise yourself for something they are involved in.

Real friends do just the opposite; they respect your beliefs and support ethical solutions to problems. They don't support unethical or stupid decisions.

Luckily I also had real friends. People who had the courage to sit down and tell me face to face why something I was doing was not in my best interests. Marty Rafferty was one of those friends.

I was supervising the Minneapolis Police Academy and was having some difficulty communicating with my Lieutenant. Marty was a manager in personnel at the time. This Lieutenant would talk very badly about Marty and the rest of the administration behind their backs, and was also causing me all sorts of grief on a daily basis. For example, on one occasion this lieutenant told me about a major policy change that was to take effect immediately. Just by chance, the Chief of Police had talked to me about the same issue the day before and I knew that what he wanted done was the exact opposite of what the lieutenant had just told me. So I went directly to the Chief, skipping three levels of command, and confirmed that he did not approve of and was not aware of any change in the policy. Of course my Lieutenant went right through the roof. The next day Marty wanted to go to lunch.

Marty saw the conflict and he reminded me that this lieutenant would probably be a chief of police some day, and she is in a smaller community. He knew what was going on behind his back. He just put it down to immaturity and reminded me of the positive skills this lieutenant possessed. Something I, in my frustration, wasn't willing to do. Marty listened to me rant for a few minutes and then said he had another meeting to go to. The next day Marty brought me a book and said, "You should read this. It's a very good book."

I read the book. It was mostly about inventory control and business management, but it also had a message about chain of command and how important it is to use the chain of command to make things run on an even keel. Marty had done it again; a strong message with a soft touch. Marty was never a cop; but there was a lot that cops could learn from this civilian and when I think about civilian input into policing I think about men like Marty Rafferty.

I would never have described Marty as a close friend. I can't recite details about his family or his recent trips, but I can tell you this. Marty Rafferty was a good friend, to me and lots of other folks. He was the kind of friend we should all try to be, and the world is a poorer place without him.

"WHEN ONE FAILS, HE FAILS US ALL."
THE CODE OF SILENCE—ACADEMY STYLE

An entire Georgia academy class fired for cheating on a test. Hard to believe? Not really. As a former academy supervisor I've seen instructors drill into recruits the message that "No one gets left behind," "We take care of own," "If one fails we all fail." I've said it myself, and I've seen the occasional disastrous results. I had to sit down and explain to two of my most promising recruits why they were being fired for trying to meet that standard. Of course by then it was too late. Like the men and women in the Georgia academy they were in shock over the consequences of their actions. They did what they thought was implied in their trainer's statements.

As trainers and supervisors, we often fail to make clear the fine line between individual accountability and group effort. We forget the power of language and the influence we have over new recruits. We assume they will understand, when what we should assume is that they understand nothing. We owe them clear expectations and direct supervision. Then, if they cross the line we know it is an ethics problem, not a supervision or communication problem. I know that some of you will argue that it's an integrity issue and they failed - their fault. Really? When was the last time you passed the "posted speed limit test," unless there was a squad car in your rear-view mirror? Where was your integrity then? Go ahead, tell me everyone drives over the speed limit. Now think about what that implies in terms of those Georgia recruits.

Compliance with the rules is not automatic, even for ethical people. Nobody knows that better than cops. We have a unique role in society, and when we introduce recruits to the police culture we need to provide a context for our remarks and an ethical foundation for ideas like "If one fails we all fail," and "We take care of our own." In addition we need to demonstrate our commitment to the true meaning of those concepts by showing them how "taking care of our own" means not allowing another cop to do something that will endanger his or her career. We need to make it clear that we will occasionally fail but that it's the fight for ethical conduct that makes us strong. It's not about whether we win or lose.

A veteran cop understands the meaning of "If one fails we all fail." The veteran cop knows that just one cop's failure to do a complete search or his failure get into the fight in time can be deadly. But the veteran cop also knows that there will be failures because we're human beings and we're prone to make mistakes. Even without mistakes a cop always has his back to someone and when some sociopath is truly committed to killing a cop, it's pretty hard to stop them.

Most importantly, a veteran cop has learned from years of experience that bad decisions made by one police officer affect all of us. In fact a veteran cop might be tempted to restate that axiom so that it reads, "When one fails, he fails us all." Even veteran street cops occasionally need supervisors to step in and make "corrections." Why would we expect recruits to be any different?

My question for the academy staff in Georgia is the same question I asked myself when I lost two promising recruits: "How could these recruits possibly think it was OK to cheat? Where did we go wrong?" I don't know if I ever came up with an answer to those questions, but I do know that losing those recruits brought home to me how important it is to explain ethical conduct in terms that can be applied on a daily basis to what they are doing. If we want our recruits to be ethical then we need to show them what that means. We can't assume that they will understand. And being "silent" about how something is to be accomplished just sets up the recruit for failure.

Law enforcement agencies spend a lot of time and money getting applicants to the point of academy training. It's not just an ethical problem for a department when they let a recruit go, it's also about the money. It's expensive to get recruits to that stage. I assume the men and women in that academy had satisfactory backgrounds and psychological test results. If there were indicators of deviant behavior I assume that they wouldn't have been hired. I hope the leadership in that department is having a long sit down with the people involved to determine what happened.

I also wonder if the physical fitness training in Georgia emphasized teamwork and success for "everyone or no one?" That's very often where the message "No one gets left behind" is emphasized the most. There are good reasons for that. You have to believe that no matter how bad it gets or how dangerous it becomes, your fellow officers will be there for you and difficult fitness training is a good place to test those men and women.

But let's get back to the real question: "Why did they think they could cheat on a test?" And the answer is "They probably didn't see it as cheating." If we can believe what the recruits are quoted as saying to the media, there was a code of silence among the academy staff to get these people through the program. I can't and won't believe that this was an entire class of unethical recruits. This was a failure at the academy level, and deliberate or not, if there was any cheating it was the academy that cheated those recruits and the code of silence – training style – is alive and well in Georgia.

WHAT DO YOU CALL AN OFFICER WHO BEATS A BRUTALITY COMPLAINT? YOUR UNION STEWARD.

It was always a joke on our department that the cops who survived clear cases of misconduct were the cops most likely to end up being our union stewards. It wasn't always true, but like any good myth it had just enough truth in it to make it seem real. There was always a board member you could point to and say "There's the proof." This was brought home recently when one of our federation representatives, who just got time off for an off-duty fight and has a fairly high number of Internal Affairs complaints, was accused by other cops of implying (in a police training venue) that Minnesota Congressman Keith Ellison was a terrorist because he was Muslim. Unbelievable! But I've seen worse.

As the supervisor of the Minneapolis Police Academy from 1994 to 1999 it fell on me to be the "expert witness" in civilian review complaints with regard to policy and procedure. I testified both for and against officers at civilian review hearings. Testimony in support of officers in order to correct a misunderstanding was always easy. Testifying against officers accused of misconduct was sometimes made much more difficult by the presence of our union stewards, known as federation representatives. It always irked me when we had an officer with a history of abuse being vigorously defended by his or her federation representative.

But like it or not those union stewards served an important purpose. Their role on the department is sort of like the role played by the bacteria in your gut. You can't go without them, but sometimes

what they do just plain stinks. If you have a perfect supervisor who
reports to a perfect commander who reports to the perfect chief
you don't need a union or a union steward. But I don't know of any
department like that and it seems like every time I thought that was
the case for me somebody did something to ruin my daydream.

I can think of two examples where a less than perfect administration on my department attempted to unfairly force terminations.
In the first one I was called upon to review and testify about the
actions of another supervisor who had been involved in a number
of excessive force cases. Over the years his version of street work
had cost the city millions of dollars in payouts for lawsuits and
now they wanted to use a relatively minor incident to terminate
him. I told the attorneys involved that I could testify, based on the
officers' reports, that this supervisor's actions were a deliberate
provocation intended to give him an excuse to use physical force.
I also told them that it was not a firing offense and that I was sure
the arbiter would never fire him for this incident. At the hearing
the supervisor was represented by a good attorney and his federation rep. They supported him, arguing about the righteousness of
his actions, the need for quick action, fast decisions, etc. The arbiter
ruled in favor of discipline and not termination. It was a fair ruling.

In the second case an officer was being charged with a whole
laundry list of conjured violations of the policy manual. A particular deputy chief wanted to punish this officer for his past history and, I believe, his associations with a gay, former Catholic
priest. The officer involved asked me to read through the file. The

charges they trumped up against him were outrageous. Some of the conclusions reached in the internal investigation were so blatantly false that the investigator must have been mentally gagging as he typed up the final report. The supervisor that reviewed and approved of the report was no better. Worst of all was the deputy chief that pushed this case through. I wrote a letter to the Chief detailing the deception and false conclusions that I found in the investigation. Most of the charges against the officer were eventually dropped.

I'm not defending the conduct of either one of these officers, but I am ready to defend against injustice when I see it and it always struck me as ironic when one of our administrators would attack a police officer for trampling on someone's rights and then be willing to do exactly the same thing to their own cop.

If you're a righteous sort of cop it would be easy to take the moral high ground in these cases and get angry about stewards who protect dirty cops. If moral justice and legal justice were the same thing we could do that. But they're not. Legal justice is about the fair application of the law, to everyone. Moral justice is an objective we can strive for, but it is met only occasionally or accidentally in the criminal justice system. In our country, moral justice and legal justice are more likely to be in conflict than agreement. If they weren't and we let moral justice rule our country, like they do some middle-eastern countries, we would be at the mercy of religious groups. And depending on which group was in power, that could be very scary. Don't misunderstand me; I'm not against religion. I'm just against religious beliefs replacing the rule of law.

The bottom line is this. As good cops who refuse to defend the actions of dirty cops we can take the moral high ground with regard to their actions. But, as good cops, and the guardians of everyone's civil rights, we must support an aggressive defense of every charge made against a cop, guilty or not. We can't let people in power think they can get away with marginalizing anyone's rights just because they have the power to do so.

The union steward, federation representative, whatever you call them, have a job to do.

We don't have to like it. We do have to support it.

THE COST OF TRAINING: A FEW DOLLARS
SAVING A LIFE: PRICELESS.

For a number of years the Minneapolis Police Department and the FBI had a joint SWAT team. The idea for a joint team came from then S.A. Al Garber, the SWAT team leader and his long time partner and friend in crime fighting S.A. Steve Gilkerson. They had a small team of highly motivated team members but the other team members lacked the background and experience that comes from working the streets in full uniform with a full array of tools at your beltline. Garber, a former Army Ranger Captain and Gilkerson a former Marine Corps Captain, both Viet Nam combat veterans, recognized the limitations of having a team with little experience in combat, unless you counted oral arguments during law school. The small size of the team also limited the scope of the team's capabilities.

Just as important, there wasn't a lot of emphasis on applying the officer survival tactics learned in SWAT training to the day to day duties of the average FBI agent. The primary emphasis at that time, prior to 9/11, was on white collar crime and serving a warrant often meant calling up the suspect and "inviting" them to come down to the office to "talk." Working with the Minneapolis cops in SWAT training, and in the relaxed conversations over a beer or two at the end of the day, those agents gained a different viewpoint on the importance of everyday officer survival tactics. It was good for the agents and it was good for the cops, but it took a lot of time off the streets for some of Minneapolis's better and more aggressive street cops.

Yesterday I had breakfast with Al and Steve. We have remained friends since the beginning of the joint SWAT team idea and we still get together pretty regularly. Our conversation was mostly about family, kids, my grandkids, prostate medicines, blood pressure medicine side effects, and the best bet for hearing aids. At one point Steve started to laugh and said, "We used to talk about sex, taking down bad guys at gun point, and SWAT tactics. Now, we've been here for two hours and not one of has even mentioned the fact that our waitress is really cute. Instead we talk about our pills. What happened to us?" We all laughed. Then Al brought up a quick change of topics.

"I've thought a lot about our joint team and what it took to get the Minneapolis cops the time off the streets to train." He said. "I would have to talk to supervisors and explain the importance of what we were doing. And their argument was that every time I took their cops to some training it was taking the better cops off the street and it was the precinct and the city that lost out. They didn't see the value of the training and they didn't like the fact that the FBI could take their cops away for two days a month, just for training. Now as I look back, I think maybe they were right and I was wrong. We didn't really use the team very much. It was mostly just training." I stopped Al right there.

"Al, I understand what you are saying, but I think you're wrong. We put on two or more SWAT schools a year for a lot of years. We trained hundreds, if not thousands, of cops in tactics that they would never get through their regular in-service training. More importantly, the vast majority of those officers were in those SWAT schools because they were the most aggressive and active street officers and they in turn became the department trainers and supervisors down the road."

"Maybe you're right." Al said Then it was time to split the check. Our breakfast had turned into two and one half hours of visiting time.

A few years back when Al was the U.S. Marshal in Minnesota he told me that we can try to change things but in the end we probably won't make much difference. Rocking the boat and pushing the limits of what we can be or should be is fine and good, but in the long run things stay pretty much the same. I found that a strange thing to hear from a man who had made such a difference in the level of tactical training for the cops in Minnesota, and North and South Dakota. I know he was referring to my book on the code of silence, but it made me think about the importance of what we do on a daily basis.

Those SWAT schools provided training, for free, to cops all over the three state region for a number of years. There is no way to measure what did not happen as a result of the training those cops received. The pause at the corner, the slicing the pie, the limited penetration shooting, the firearms skills, basic crisis negotiations, weapon retention, disarming techniques, high risk stops, and a hundred other tactics that cops use to stay alive were taught, improved upon, and passed on to generations of cops in this area. And I know that it saved lives, and it made a difference.

Bean counters will always be concerned about measuring the upfront costs on everything. If they can't measure it they don't count it and you can't measure or show your city manager the savings in lives that aren't lost. Maybe there is a price to pay up front and maybe we have to argue, cajole or even beg for our training time, but if that's what you have to do then do it. The cost of training: a few dollars. Saving a life: priceless.

I DON'T CARE HOW YOU GET IT DONE! JUST DO IT! ONE OF THE WORST THINGS A SUPERVISOR CAN SAY TO A COP.

"The cops I work with will do what you tell them. . . . But don't look, you don't want to watch." That quote from "Rampart Reconsidered" is found on page 4 of the appendices section. It is attributed to an LAPD supervisor with more than 25 years experience in the LAPD. There is another quote on page 12 in the same report attributed to Deputy Chief Paysinger. It reads: "Because if you ask too much they'll deliver for you. But you won't want to know how they got the result." There are seemingly endless quotes in the report that talk about the code of silence, the ends justify the means sort of policing, lack of supervision, lack of administrative backing, etc., etc., etc. It's worthwhile going to the LAPD website and downloading the reports for yourself.

You could spend years talking about what's wrong with the LAPD and how Rampart got so out of hand. But I also know there is a lot right with the LAPD. Just read the comments made by supervisors and commanders in the Rampart report and you realize that there are a lot of men and women on that department that care about what is happening to the LAPD street officers and the community they serve. The department is an enigma. Perhaps the best description I ever heard of the LAPD was "They are the best and the worst department in the world." I think I know what he meant. We look to LAPD for the best in training, in SWAT, and in new tactics. And we look to LAPD for the worst case scenarios of what cops can do wrong, and we're not surprised when we find it. That's why I wasn't surprised to learn that turning cops loose, without supervision, to decide how to get the job done resulted in ". . . you don't want to watch."

I had a couple of supervisors that were quick to tell me about problems they wanted fixed, without any reports. These gutless men, and one woman, were also the first supervisors to stand up and say

"I never told him to do that. I would never and have never told any officer to do anything illegal" when something went wrong.

Later in my career, as recruits passed through the academy I tried to impress upon them the importance of clear direction and goals. I'm not talking about mission statements or department objectives. Those are important too if they give clear direction and they're not all gobbledeegook political correctness. I am talking about giving clear direction to your subordinates when there is a problem to address. For instance: You have drunks loitering in a specific area of the city and the mayor is getting complaints from the Downtown Business Alliance.

I remember a similar problem in Minneapolis and I remember a supervisor who told me to look at the problem from a citizen stand-point and then come back with some ideas on what might work or at least appease the business alliance. Most importantly, report back to him, before I took any action. What a great boss! The best part was that after we came up with some ideas the sergeant supported a couple of them and he helped us with the resources we needed to get the job done. If things didn't go as planned he was the first to step up and say it was a plan he approved.

If you are asking yourself what any of this has to do with police ethics you may be one of those supervisors who routinely asks the people working for him or her to "just get it done." In your defense it's likely that you received the typical less-than-inspiring supervisory training and no one ever showed you any other way to do it.

It's also possible that your supervisors always abdicated their responsibilities in the name of getting along or police discretion so that's the only supervisory model you know. It's even more likely that there are very strong informal leaders in the ranks below you and if you don't go along with their program you end up looking like the bad guy. Too bad, you are no longer one of the troops; you are a supervisor, so act like one.

You not only have the authority, you have the responsibility, to give direction to the men and women who work for you. When you give orders without direction the officers working for you have two ways of interpreting your action. They will believe that you either 1) don't care how they get it done as long as it doesn't come back to bite you or 2) that you are clueless. Think about that.

It will seem like you are getting along better because you are leaving it up to them but you're not really. If they think of you as mindless they will keep you in the dark, and you will never know what is happening on the street. It will seem like everything is going along just fine, which should be an immediate red flag. If they think of you as gutless they will never come to you with the tough decisions they are contemplating. Which one do you prefer? You owe it to them, as a supervisor, to tell them what you want done, how you want it done, and when you want it done or you should take off your stripes.

Cops make mistakes and there's no better way to set up a cop for a big fall than giving them a tough problem without direction. If the cops on your shift are failing to produce or are drawing more complaints than they should it is your problem as much as theirs.

You should want to know how your cops are getting the job done. You should be able to take pride in how they do it. And don't ever tell a subordinate to "just get it done and I don't want to know how you do it." That's a coward's way out. I'm pretty sure that if you made it to a supervisory level you are not a coward so don't act like one.

A LETTER TO THE MINNEAPOLIS STAR TRIBUNE: KEEP UP THE GOOD WORK

For many years the *Minneapolis Star Tribune,* like a lot of metropolitan newspapers, reported on police activities as if the Minneapolis cops were the bad guys and every mistake or misstep by a cop was an act of malfeasance. Not that the Minneapolis cops were always innocent, but most of them did, and still do, their job with courage, honor, and integrity. You wouldn't have known how good they really were because the news media went out of its way to beat us up in print every chance it got. But things are changing here in Minneapolis. The *Star Tribune* has new owners, and it shows.

Over that the past few weeks I've seen more positive articles about our cops than I saw in the last few years combined. That's not to say the cops should or will be on a perpetual honeymoon with the press. The community needs to know about deliberate police misconduct and what the department is doing to hold these cops accountable. Accountability is important on many levels. Appropriate sanctions, from verbal warnings to days off, are often a wakeup call that serves to prevent future misconduct. I know it worked for me, more than once, and I saw it work for others as well. And, except for those cases of extreme misconduct, nobody wants a cop to lose their job. We need them and we want our cops back on the street as soon as possible.

But when the press restricts its role with regard to the cops as that of a sanctioning agent the public gets a grossly distorted view of the cops. Good policing requires citizen involvement. That's no secret to a cop. It's a symbiotic relationship. Neither can survive without the other. Everything from neighborhood crime prevention to information on a recent homicide comes out of the community. You can be the best super sleuth in the world and it won't help one bit if the community won't work with you. That means the citizens have to trust their cops; but they won't when the only thing the community sees in the press is reports of police misconduct, real and alleged.

Negative reporting, without some realistic balance, pits the cops against the community and the community against the cops. It's bad for the cops and it's bad for the community.

The written word, especially in a major newspaper, is an incredibly powerful weapon when it is used as such. It attacks without fear of retaliation and it never needs to apologize because there is almost always at least a glimmer of truth in what it prints. It can destroy in a thousand words relationships that took years for a police department to put together and the media has no regrets, because it sells newspapers. But there is another way. When the press is willing, it can be a powerful agent of peace and cooperation. It can bring the cops and community together. It can build bridges instead of walls; and that's good for the community and it's good for the cops.

I always knew how destructive the press could be but it wasn't until recently, when I felt the emotional impact of those positive police stories in the Star Tribune that I was reminded of how deep my frustration ran with the constant negative press.

The Minneapolis Police Department has struggled for a long time in its efforts to build a strong police-community relationship in the face of constant criticism, a problem we don't see in our sister city St. Paul. If we go back a few years we see the perfect example of how different we are from St. Paul. In 1992 Minneapolis Police Officer Jerry Haaf is assassinated by cowardly gang members; shot in the back while on his dinner break. I rode in the funeral procession, along with hundreds of other cops, and it was a wonderful service but the procession and the service were attended by mostly cops.

Skip ahead to August 1994. St. Paul Officers Ron Ryan Jr., Tim Jones and his K-9 partner Laser are killed by Guy Harvey Baker. During the funeral procession I rode in a Minneapolis squad car and saw block after block after block of citizens with signs saying things like "We love you." and "Thank you St. Paul Police." I don't think we went a single block through the entire miles long procession that there wasn't someone standing on the sidewalk expressing their gratitude and their sadness for the loss of those officers.

There is only the ribbon of water called the Mississippi separating Minneapolis and St. Paul physically, but there is a gulf separating us in the way we are perceived by our communities; we can thank the press for that.

I can only hope the Minneapolis Star Tribune continues to provide us with the real stories about the great work done being done every day by the investigators and street cops of the Minneapolis Police Department. I'm not asking for sugar coating, just fair and honest reporting.

Here is my appeal to the editors of the *Minneapolis Star Tribune:* You Have the Power. We all know that. You're like a laser that can instantly cut and burn. In the right hands it is a tool of healing. In the wrong hands it is an instrument of destruction. Help us to heal the police community relationship in Minneapolis. What you have done in your recent reporting on cops is wonderful. Keep up the good work. You can make a difference.

LETTER TO A NEW CHIEF
AND EVERY OTHER CHIEF LAW ENFORCEMENT OFFICER
OUT THERE!

Tim Dolan is the new Chief of Police in Minneapolis, and I'm glad. Tim is a former partner of mine. He was a good partner and when he was promoted and became my boss he was a good boss. I know that Tim loves cops and that no matter how high up he goes in the chain of command he will always be a cop, and a good man. I know that he is also a devoted dad and husband with a gentle, forgiving side that not many people have seen. I am happy for him, but I don't envy him. He has taken on what may be the toughest job in the state. Violent crime in Minneapolis is higher than it should be given what's happening in the rest of the U.S. With the murders and gang shootings occurring in our poorest, and most crime ridden areas many of the citizens have lost faith in our cops. Not because we have bad cops, but because our citizens are having a hard time seeing cops as part of their community.

Minneapolis cops are crime fighters and they work hard but it's no secret that the police can only do so much and they can't be held responsible for the root causes of crime. Lack of education, under-employment, and dysfunctional families have more of an impact on crime than the total number of cops responding to calls for service.

We are and probably always will be primarily a reactive service, and the higher the crime rate, the more calls for service and with more calls for service there is less time for proactive, community policing efforts. Whether it's POP, COP, SARA, or Broken Windows, you can't connect with the community in any meaningful way if your whole shift is spent running from call to call. In fact, it's more likely that when the cops are pushed like this they will feel like an occupation force trying to keep the lid on opposing forces over which they have little or no control. And that's not too far from the truth.

In our relatively crime free neighborhood of Southwest Minneapolis my neighbors talk about the north side of the city as a "war zone" that should be "fenced off" from the rest of the city; as if that will protect our little corner of the world from the violence. These perceptions, like the lie that is partially true, have enough truth in each of them to make them powerful forces in an argument for excusing or justifying police behavior that we would not tolerate in other times or other parts of the city.

There are lots of good cops, working very hard, in very tough conditions, in cities all across North America. And it's incredibly frustrating to cops, and the citizens under siege in those bad neighborhoods, when their best efforts don't seem to even make a dent in the problems we face. It would be easy in times like these for Chief Dolan and his commanders to turn a blind eye to infractions committed "in the heat of battle," but it would also be a grave mistake. Excessive force, creative report writing, racial profiling, and hiding behind the code of silence are wrong when times are good and they are just as wrong when times are tough.

We must expect our cops be at their best when the events and circumstances surrounding them are at their worst. The community should be able to depend on them to show the restraint, courage, compassion, and control that are missing in the lives of so many folks. In addition, they should be held accountable when they don't. The community needs examples of what can be possible, not what is excusable, and Chief Dolan can and should lead the way. He should be reminding his cops that their conduct or misconduct are very often the reason behind a community's willingness or lack thereof to share what it knows about the crimes going on all around them. Spokespersons for the Minneapolis Police Department have repeatedly had to publicly ask for help in solving crimes that should have had citizens volunteering information within minutes of the crime being made public. Instead we hear our public relations people lament the fact that: "There are people who know what happened but they aren't coming forward with the information."

It's a matter of trust Chief. When citizens trust their cops the phones in homicide will be ringing off the hook with tips concerning major crimes, and you will gain that trust when you hold them accountable for misconduct. It would also help in your communications with those neighborhoods under siege if you make your record of accountability public, like so many other agencies have done. If you did that you could have more impact on solving the gang and murder problem than any police strategy you could devise. The citizens have placed their trust in you. As your former partner and a citizen in your city I trust you will do what's right by the community and the cops. Demand courage, compassion, control, and restraint from your cops. Your community will understand mistakes by cops, but they will expect accountability. Take that first step. The community wants to trust you as much as I do.

MY NEW YEAR'S RESOLUTION
AN UNEXPECTED ACT OF KINDNESS.

This is the time of year to give thanks for all our blessings and make plans for the New Year. As I write this column my Grandson, Devon, is sitting a few feet away playing a computer game. He is a happy young man of 9 years. He is attending a public fine-arts grade school with small classes and very devoted teachers. He lives in a nice home in a good neighborhood. His Dad, my son-in-law, is a wonderful man. He is kind, gentle, gainfully employed, and everything a father-in-law could ever wish for; and until his year-old daughter Alora gets married, he will never know how thankful I am that he found my daughter. My wife is working as an RN in a county clinic that services a primarily Hispanic and illegal alien clientele. Many of her patients come to the U.S. because they have disease processes that they cannot get treated for in their own country due to the cost or in some cases just a lack of available services. My wife loves working as a nurse; a career she started only 4 years ago. I am grateful that there will be healthier children as a result of our county's policies toward everyone. So life is good, today.

We are your basic white middle class couple and it was only a few years ago that my daughter was a single mom with a mixed-race child. My cop cynicism saw only a lonely future and hard days ahead for her. But it was a cynicism born out of my experience with the world of policing and I should have trusted that everything would work out. She is smart, like her mother, and that mistake may have changed her world, but it didn't change the person she was. She is a wonderful Mom and my Grandchildren are the love of my life.

It was only a little over a year ago that my wife was diagnosed with breast cancer and underwent a mastectomy. It was a dark time for both of us and once again I let my cynicism get the best of me as I envisioned only worst case scenarios for months after the surgery. Chemo wasn't an option because of some other medical complications (a mixed blessing) so she went with the one therapy available to her. Her odds are only very slightly worse than if she had undergone chemo, but at the time it seemed like a big deal.

As we entered the Christmas Season I stopped to think about what was important to me and as always my wife wanted to know what my New Year's resolutions would be. I didn't have any at the time but as I took time to think about the last few years I decided that the first thing I was going to do was try to eliminate that cynicism that comes out of years of seeing only the worst in people and planning for worst case scenarios. I started by remembering how very lucky I am to have such a wonderful son-in-law and two beautiful grandchildren. I know that my wife and I are extremely lucky to have found her tumor when we did since it had not been picked up on her last mammogram. I am grateful that we live in a country that doesn't measure a person's eligibility for medical care by the color of their skin or their immigration status and I am grateful that we provide the prenatal care necessary for the health expectant mothers.

My cynicism for the whole issue of illegal immigration is now reserved for our professional politicians and their political power plays that do nothing to solve the problem.

Enough rambling. Cynicism is understandable when you've worked the streets for any length of time, but it is also counterproductive. It's easy to see the problems and list all the negative fallout that will result. The thing is, most of the time we don't experience the worst case scenario. Most of the time things work out OK. Crime rates for example. A few years ago when every criminologist in the world was predicting a crime wave of immeasurable proportions we prepared for the worst, and it didn't happen. In fact, crime went down. Nobody seems to know why. It just did.

We prepare, or at least we should prepare, for a worst case scenario every time we make a high-risk entry or respond to a domestic call. In most cases we are over-prepared, and that's OK in terms of officer survival but it also contributes to our cynicism.

Physically we prepare ourselves for the confrontation that we know will occur. We work out hard; we try to reach our pain threshold in training so we can tolerate it when we are challenged on the street. Yet, we are only involved in physical confrontations about 2% of the time. And most of those are minor uses of force. But the idea is still in our head that we need to be ready for the worst and unless we are careful that's how we end up viewing the world. In preparing for the worst we lose sight of the best things that are coming our way. We forget how to prepare ourselves to see the good in what's happening around us and in that idea I found a reason for my New Year's resolution.

We live in a cynical world. We are in a cynical profession, maybe the most cynical of professions. But in our profession we also have the opportunity to make it a brighter and better world for those around us, and by doing that we can brighten our own world. My New Year's resolution is to engage in one act of unexpected kindness every day. Maybe we can't change the world, but we can change moments in time, and that may be the most important.

WHAT WE DO "TO" PEOPLE IS NECESSARY.
WHAT WE DO "FOR" PEOPLE IS WHAT MAKES IT
WORTHWHILE.

I have been looking to get back into full-time policing, and I have
been asking myself "Why?" I have been retired since 1999 from the
police department, after 23 years, and I left my part-time gig with
the U.S. Marshal's Service a couple months ago. I mentioned this at
breakfast last week with my two retired FBI friends. I didn't mention that I was feeling some internal stress about whether I could
"cut it" again. Both of them are long-time SWAT, fugitive task force
commanders, and Viet Nam vets. Somehow, without mentioning
my concerns, we got on the topic of the stages cops go through in
their careers and how the locker room rhetoric changes with years
and experience levels.

Al remarked that the young cops are filled with bravado and
a sense of invulnerability. Taking down the next bad guy, winning
a physical confrontation, going to that next man with a gun call,
and getting into a major pursuit are all these young officers want
to do. As he talked I remembered when I was like that. In fact,
when my friends think I am being too critical of police officers and
some of the bad choices they make, they are quick to remind me of
just how wild, crazy, and fearless I was in my younger years; and
they are right. The key word here is "fearless," often synonymous
with "brainless." You did not, and you will not, see me use the
word brave. In my early years I often I created more danger by my
actions, not less.

By way of example: As a young officer I watched as senior officers took more time to approach people and calls, evaluating and planning, while I responded by jumping into the middle of the fray. I went through a lot of good, experienced partners because I was quick to criticize their hesitancy. I saw it as a reluctance to act. When they criticized me for not waiting for them I thought of them as "retired on the job" because they did not want to run down that dark alley to chase everyone who fled from them. I would complain about their reluctance to get into vehicle pursuits and call them "old lady drivers." I found a million and one reasons to complain about their work and their work ethic. I was one of the "New Centurions," the professional police officer, and things were going to be different when all these old guys retired.

Then they retired, and things were different, because now I was the old guy. Now I was taking time to evaluate and plan a little before I responded. I began to question the justification for no-knock warrants that seldom recovered anything of significance. All my hard charging, risk taking, and putting other officers at risk hadn't change a thing in terms of the crime rate. Strangely enough, there were still drive-by shootings, husbands still beating their wives, rapists still victimizing women, drunk drivers still killing people on a daily basis, and there were still senseless acts of cruelty being acted out every day. And I began to question why I was doing this job.

When I started in law enforcement I was told two things; 1) That at about seven years I would become a seasoned officer and 2) That somewhere between 7 and 11 years on the job, I would question my choice of careers and most likely be divorced. I was also told that at that point I would probably drop the idea of making any real difference and start viewing police work as a job; eight for eight, or eight for whatever I could get away with. I believed those trainers and when I started wondering about my choice of careers, I examined mine within those parameters and found that there was no resolution. I think that's because I was asking the wrong questions.

For a long time I tried to do the job better each day and then I started to question myself. I was witness to crime scenes that would make me cry when I got home at night. I still remember the broken bodies of babies killed by those who were supposed to protect them, the bullet holes and blood splattered walls over the bodies of innocents, and the voice of a crying mother on the phone who was half a world away, when I told her that her daughter was dead by her own hand. I couldn't stop any of those acts. At best, I was a witness to the depths of despair and depravity of which mankind is capable, and I had to make a decision to either go on with this job or quit. I stayed, but before I made that decision I had to ask myself, "Why?"

As I saw it I had at least three choices: 1) I could choose to stay on the street and be as vicious and hard and cruel as the bad guys; throw ethics out the window and make cases any way I could. 2) I could choose to retire on the job and find a nice cozy place where I shuffled papers, away from the street and any contact with victims or suspects. Or, 3) I could make a decision to stay on the job and rededicate myself to being ethical but relentless in the pursuit of the bad guys. I gave up the idea of trying to change the world by locking up every bad guy. That's not going to happen.

I came to realize that I could work hard with the idea that if I do this job well there will be one less victim and one less nightmare for the survivors. That made it worth staying. In this job we do "to" some people and we do "for" others. What we do "to" people is necessary. What we do "for" people is what makes it worthwhile. I looking forward to doing "for" people again.

DUTY, HONOR, COUNTRY.
COURAGE, COMPASSION, JUSTICE.

On May 12, 1962, General Douglas MacArthur gave his farewell speech to the graduating cadets at West Point. His speech was simple and profound. I quote part of it here: "Duty, Honor, Country—those three hallowed words reverently dictate what you want to be, what you can be, what you will be."

My brother Hugh is in Iraq. He has been in the military a long time. Like many of the soldiers over there, he left behind a wife and two teenage girls who miss him very much. He didn't want to go to war. He sure didn't want to leave his wife and girls. But he knew that when he was called he would go. He understands Duty, Honor, Country. He took an oath and he is living by that oath.

Back here in the civilian world, The Law Enforcement Code of Ethics is an oath many of us have sworn to uphold. I don't know that there are three words that can adequately represent the Code but I am going to try—Courage, Compassion, Justice. I beg your indulgence in this endeavor because like General MacArthur stated, I don't have the words or the abilities to say all that those words mean to me. I do believe that like Duty, Honor, Country, these words also represent "what you want to be, what you can be, what you will be."

When I was a young cop I wanted to be viewed as courageous by my peers and my friends. I wanted to be involved in the big gun fight, the one-on-one hand to hand fight with a bigger opponent, and the car chase that topped 100 mph and ended in the capture of the FBI's most wanted person. I wanted crooks to fear me and neighborhoods to be at peace because I was on patrol. I thought that's what courage was about. But that's not courage, that's just recklessness; something common to young men and women. Some of the best police work wouldn't happen without it; just don't mistake it for courage.

It took me some time but I learned that courage in law enforcement isn't about physical courage. It's about standing up for what's right; it's about doing the right thing for the right reasons, even when the consequences for you will be bad.

But I didn't come to these realizations in a vacuum. I had partners and supervisors who took me aside and sometimes gently, and sometimes not so gently, reminded me of my obligations to them (first of all), then to my family and the citizens. They didn't mention the "oath." They didn't have to; they lived it. Compassion for people of all races and a sense of justice for even the lowest levels of humanity were more than just part of the job, they were the heart and soul of how these officers lived. And now I have a brother who is living his oath of Duty, Honor, Country and once again I am reminded of the importance of the Law Enforcement Code of Ethics, and the meaning of justice.

There is a tendency to equate "Justice" with moral justice, and it just isn't true. Criminal justice is a question of applying the law to a set of facts. If there is fair representation at a court of law there's justice. It doesn't matter if an innocent man is convicted of a crime he didn't commit or a guilty man goes free. We apply the law and supposedly everyone gets a fair shot at "justice." But real justice, community justice, doesn't come from the law. It comes from individual acts of compassion and justice by individual officers. And I'm not talking about "street justice." Street justice is an act committed by thugs, usually cowards. This gets me back to our starting point.

There are around 130,000 U.S. troops in Iraq. Men and women who are living their oath of Duty, Honor, Country and they are giving their lives, their limbs, and their families for their country; for us. They don't refuse to fight because they don't believe in the war or the politics that started it, or any of the other BS that cops use to justify testilying, creative report writing, or acts of violence. They fight and they die because they swore an oath to protect us. You did the same. You swore an oath to "protect the innocent against oppression or intimidation and the peaceful against violence or disorder; and to respect the Constitutional rights of all men to liberty, equality, and justice."

Don't dishonor the men and women who fight for our country and are living up to their oath to protect us all. Live up to your oath. Whether it's Duty, Honor, Country or Courage, Compassion, Justice - it's time to step up.

Note—Brother Hugh returned safely from Iraq a few months after this column ran.

WHAT REALLY MATTERS?
A TOUGH WEEK IN MINNEAPOLIS

Police training and equipment has only gotten better over the years and for the most part we can prepare ourselves for what this job is going to throw at us. The man with a knife may be a surprise, but if we've trained for it we will have a response that should reduce our risk of being stabbed or killed. The unknown trouble, the 911 hang-up, the violent domestic, the high-speed pursuit – we can prepare ourselves in terms of our skills and our attitudes. But how do you prepare for the time when you accidentally kill one of your own? I don't know how to answer that question, and I desperately want to answer that question because it's happened again, and this time it was someone I knew.

I know Minneapolis isn't the only place this kind of tragedy has happened this year, or in previous years. Law enforcement nationwide has seen far too many accidental deaths in the last few months; the majority of them involving motor vehicles. Mark Bedard's death was no exception.

Mark was one of my recruits. I say that with a sense of pride. As the supervisor of the Minneapolis Academy I was proud of the way the staff (my partners in this endeavor) prepared the recruits for the street with a big dose of officer survival training moderated by some sense of their limitations. He wasn't the first of my recruits to be killed in the line of duty, but this one was different because Mark was run over by another Minneapolis Police officer who was responding to help him. An accident for sure, but in many ways that makes it worse.

There is nothing we can do for Mark at this point. He's in the hands of his God, and knowing Mark, I'm sure he's in a better place. There is something we can do for each other. First of all we can say a prayer for the officers that were in the car that struck Mark. I'm not a religious man. When I do go in a church I look for the lightening to strike, but I do on occasion say a prayer and those officers need our prayers; because on any given night – that could have been us behind the wheel. Most of us drive too fast and it's only luck that we get away with it.

We are supposed to take care of each other so that we all go home at night. I know it's not possible, but that's never stopped me from trying before and I know lots of Minneapolis cops that think the word impossible is spelled "I'm Possible." These are the same cops who have never used the words "quit" or "give up" unless they are yelling a command.

Mark was one of those cops. He never quit. He fought till the end. He was a wonderful man. He was a great big teddy bear of a guy with an infectious smile and a gentle touch, and he's gone. And he leaves behind a young widow and a two year old son who also need our prayers and support as they try to make sense out of this senseless tragedy.

None of us will get out of this life alive, and maybe I'm getting old in my way of thinking. Thirty years ago I was willing to take incredible risks that I wouldn't even consider now. Maybe it's because I have children, and grandchildren, that I take more time to hold them and tell them I love them. I never end a conversation with family anymore without saying, "I love you," because I realize now, more than ever, that I may not get to say that to them again. They matter to me in ways I can't express.

Look at the officers killed in the last few months; many of them were responding to calls at high speed. Where is our indignation at the senseless loss of life? Where is the partner that says "Slow down. I want to go home tonight?" What's really important in your life? Do you take unnecessary risks with your life, and the lives of other cops in the name of policing? I'm not asking you to give up the courageous acts and I realize that us old guys need the young blood of enthusiasm to keep reminding us of why we took this job in the first place. I'm just asking you to take a minute to think about what's really important. That squad car is a deadly weapon and we are killing ourselves with it just as effectively as a 9 mm round from our own weapon. And like the accidental discharge from our handgun, it's preventable, and it needs to stop.

Like I said earlier, none of us will get out of this alive. What are you doing in your off time? Are you watching your kids play sports, maybe even coaching, or are you working three part-time jobs so can afford that new boat or oversized SUV? Do you think your kids are going to remember what a great boat you had or will they remember spending time with you? Are you spending time with your spouse or life-partner, or are you partying with your work partners? Until someone proves otherwise I have to believe we only get one shot at this, no pun intended. Take time for the things that really matter and Stay Safe.

THEY'RE NEVER AROUND WHEN YOU NEED THEM.
I WISH I COULD HAVE BEEN THERE.

The collapse of the 35W Bridge in Minneapolis was awful, but it could have been much worse. There would have been many more deaths if not for the bravery of the citizens, cops, firefighters, and other rescue workers that crawled, climbed, and jumped into the twisted wreckage. That response, to put their own lives at risk in order to save a stranger, reminded me of why I became a cop; To Protect and Serve. The "serve" part being a necessary part of the job, while the "PROTECT!" mandate inspired me to choose policing over the job of paramedic. It was not an easy choice, since I had been an emergency room medic in the U.S.A.F. for the two years prior. Now, after 30 years or so of policing, police training, U.S. Marshal's service, and federal building security, I still think I made the right choice.

When the bridge collapsed I was in middle of teaching a college class. My first thought was, "Why wasn't I there to help?" For a fleeting instant my gut reaction was to jump in my car and race to the scene. An impossible idea since I was at least 45 minutes away, in the middle of a class, and I knew there would be no way to even get close to the scene by then. I also knew that the city would respond, like it always did, with heroic efforts by citizens and emergency services people alike. I don't know who said it first but it is true that, "We are often at our best when things are at their worst." That is the true nature of the human species and I knew there would be people doing whatever they could at the scene. And I knew I had to stay where I was.

Several days after the disaster my students were having a lively discussion about police discretion and traffic control on our highways. One student commented that every time she commits a minor violation the cops always seem to be right behind her but when she sees people driving like maniacs on the freeway there is never a cop around. She said, "It's so frustrating. They're never around when you need them." My wife would call this moment in time a "teaching moment." My favorite teacher, Bill Mamel, would call this an "Aha!" moment. It was, in fact, a point in time when my mind was flooded with scenes of murder, senseless vehicle fatalities, and vicious domestic violence that may have been prevented if only someone, like a cop, had been in the right place at the right time to stop it.

I paused for a moment and then I stopped the discussion and directed my comments to the student expressing her frustration and I told her, "You need to know that the frustration you feel is the same frustration the cops feel when they realize that they can't be in the right place at the right time each and every time they should be. Cops want to protect, it just can't always be done." I went on to tell the class about my first reaction to the bridge collapse. I told them about seeing Peter Erickson, a retired paramedic, at the grocery store and our shared sense of "Need to be there to help/Grateful that we're not."

I must have come across pretty strong with the student, because the mood of the class changed and the discussions were a lot more subdued after that. I got the feeling that they were afraid of what I would say next.

There is a phenomenon called survivors guilt that describes the guilt survivors feel when others around them die, and they survive. There is another type of guilt that isn't expressed very often but is very real. I call it, "Should have been there guilt." Cops occasionally talk about it, but most of the time they talk around it with comments like "That lucky bastard is always in the right place at the right time." We're jealous and frustrated even when we know that being in the right place at the right time means placing ourselves in extreme danger. Occasionally, we all have a shift where we seem to be right where we're needed, but not that often. All too often we go home with the leftover feelings of guilt and frustration because we weren't there; we could have been there; we wanted to be there, and we weren't.

Every day there is another article in the StarTribune and

another story on the local news channels about the bridge, the heroes, the victims, and the aftermath.

And every day, I wish I could have been there.

DEAR CHILDREN—
I WON'T BE HOME FOR A LONG, LONG TIME.

This last column is not the last column I wrote but I have placed it at the end because for too many of us this is how the dream ends.

Every year there are more cops going to prison than there are getting killed by felons. Many of them leave devastated families in their wake. I have often wondered if any of them took the time to think about what they could lose as a result of their misconduct. So, for a portion of the final exam in my Ethics in Criminal Justice class I had each student pretend they were a police officer convicted and sentenced to a long prison term. I asked them to write a letter to their children about what happened. I admit to getting a little teary eyed as I read over some of them. One student found herself crying halfway through the paper. I have never, as a street supervisor or academy supervisor, asked the officers or recruits to do anything I haven't done, so I sat down and composed my own letter. Emotions run deep when you think about all that you might give up when you violate the oath you took as a police officer. I challenge you to take this final exam, and then tell me that "The ends justify the means" is worth it. Here's my letter. I thank God that it's only a test. For far too many it's a reality.

Dear Children,

Writing to you today is probably the most difficult thing I've ever done. I know your mother told you already that I won't be coming home for some time. I wish I could say I was going to war or doing something important. I wish it was for anything other than what it really is. I am in prison.

I don't really know when it all started. When I was a new cop, I was told that certain rules were meant to be broken and that cops always stood up for other cops, no matter what. My supervisors and training officers all told me to forget what I learned at the academy and just keep my ears open and my mouth shut until I learned how real police work was done. I thought they were telling me the truth. Now I know different.

I already miss holding your littlest sister. I miss the way she was just learning to kiss and hug. I miss her sour milk breath, her saggy diapers, and the way she dances to your rock music. I miss the way she looked into my eyes, with complete love and absolute trust, a trust I've broken before she is even old enough to say "Daddy."

I miss you my son and I don't know how to ask for your forgiveness, but I won't be at any of your hockey games. I know we had plans for hunting and fishing this fall, but you will be out of high school and done with college before I get out of here and I will probably never be able to hunt with you again. Things will be especially hard for you because you are now the man of the house. My name will be in all the papers with a story about how I was convicted of a terrible crime. People will be cruel. They will visit the sins of the father onto the son, and for that I am truly sorry. You don't have to defend me to others. The crime is real. I did all those things, but please don't hate me.

I have no excuse, but I want you to know that I am still the same man that loved to rock you to sleep as a child and carry you on my shoulders when you were too tired to walk. When you were sick I would strip you down to your diaper and lay you on my bare chest so you could listen to my heartbeat when you put your head down. I would lie awake for hours, afraid to move, less I roll you off of me. Now, when I can't sleep at night, I pretend I am back in my own bed and you are once again a baby lying on my chest, and for a few hours I am at peace. You have plenty of good reasons to hate me at this moment but know that I will always love you.

I know you've talked about being a cop when you grow up. Don't let my mistakes turn you away from policing if that's what you really want to do. It's a great career. If you do follow in my footsteps, please forgive me long enough to grant me one wish: Be true to what you know is right. Don't let others set the rules for you. Others will tell you that the rules change as you get older or wiser. That it's OK to lie to get the job done. But that's the real lie and it will always be a lie. I love you.

My darling daughter, I can still smell that perfume you bought for your first date. You looked so beautiful I cried when you left that night. Your mother thought I had completely lost it, but I realized as you left that you were growing up and that before long another man, a stranger to me, would be the one to make you laugh when you were sad, to hold you when you cried, to pick you up when you fell, and I felt this terrible loss. Now I am lost to you by my own doing and my heart aches in ways I can't even describe as I think of all the promises I made to you that are now broken. I hurt so bad inside that I try to quit breathing, hoping that I will lose consciousness and stop the agony, but I am kept awake and alive by the demons of shame and remorse. I know that the pain I feel won't take away the pain I have caused you and I can only say, "I am sorry."

Your mother loves me and I know that she has forgiven me, but I will be gone a long time. I don't want her to be lonely and I ask you to be a friend to her when she finds someone she can laugh with again. She is a relatively young woman. She needs a man in her life, and it can't be me.

Goodbye children, I love you all, and I am so sorry,

This final piece was written by my father while he was working for Minnesota Safe and Sober. It is addressed to peace officers, but it applies to us all. So here it is Dad. I know you and Mom are still watching over us. You are finally a published author.

To My Fellow Police Officers
By William Bernard Quinn—
December 24, 1927–November 12, 2009.

The little Indian boy's body lies near the center of the intersection. The head is split open like a melon. The contents lay on the street mixed with the blood that is pooling around him. The ambulance is at the scene with an intern and a nurse in attendance. The intern says in a panicky voice, "Let's get him to the hospital." The nurse says, "Doctor, he's dead. There is nothing we can do. Call the M.E." We put a sheet over him and I approach the spectators asking if anyone knows who he is. All I know is that he looks to be Indian. No one knows him until I reach an Indian man standing alone who responds, "He is my son." I tell him how sorry I am and get the boys name and other appropriate information. I say the appropriate things and go on with my work.

I am in control.

The twelve-year-old boy's body lies in the street in front of his home. The facial features are unrecognizable as a result of the dual wheels of a heavily-laden truck running over his head as he was face up. Again the head is terribly fractured with the contents in the street. The father is screaming at everyone to do something. The mother is crying and screaming. The neighbors are in a state of shock. The ambulance crew arrives, takes one look and says, "Bill, we can't take him. He's dead." I reply, "I know that but his father just ran over him and the mother saw it happen. Get him out of here." They load him up and head for the hospital with the parents following. I ask a neighbor to wash the blood out of the street before the parents return.

I am in control.

Cindy, a seven year old, follows her sister crossing the street, and just as she is about to step up on the curb, a hit-and-run driver, who is speeding and driving like an idiot, plasters Cindy on the front bumper of his car, like a squashed butterfly. Then, according to witnesses, he jerks the vehicle to the left and Cindy flies off into the snowbank, 150 feet from where he hit her. It happened so quickly the older sister does not realize what has happened and is standing on the sidewalk saying, "Cindy? Where is Cindy?" Another motorist chases the hit-and-run vehicle and a neighbor who saw it happen picks up Cindy from the snowbank. I take her from his arms and lay her on the back seat of squad and start CPR. She is not breathing. I work on her until the ambulance arrives but I know it is useless. Her body is like a rag doll and her blood fills my mouth as I try to get some air into her. The ambulance arrives and takes her away. We process the scene. *I am in control.*

A mother running for the house carrying the body of her two-and-half-year-old daughter in her arms screaming, "She's dead!

She's dead!" The child has just been struck by a car. I take the child from her, lay her on the floor, and start CPR. She is not breathing. I have a great deal of trouble getting her airway open. Other children of the same family, friends of the children, and the mother are all screaming, praying, and crying. I hear sirens coming and another officer says, "Bill, don't stop. Keep going." There is mass confusion. I can't get any air into her. The noise of the sirens, the screaming, the shouting, the hysterical crying. I think, "This can't be happening. I have died and gone to hell." Reality could not be this bad. This is my youngest child, my daughter, that I am working on. *I am not in control.*

I finally start her breathing. The ambulance takes her to the hospital. A neighbor drives my wife and I to the hospital, but we know there is little hope. I have seen so many. She dies in surgery about an hour later.

No one washed down the street. I saw the blood stains each time I walked down the street for the next 13 years. I moved away from Minneapolis in 1983. Two weeks ago, nineteen years after we moved, I drove by our old house. The stains are still there. They will always be there. In the past year, four of our fellow officers have lost children in traffic accidents. Yes, it happens to us too. When it does, we realize *we are not in control.*

Notes

1 Crime and Victim Statistics.2009. U.S. Department of Justice, Office of Justice Programs. Retrieved on 01/12/2011, from http://bjs.ojp.usdoj.gov/index.cfm?ty=pbdetail&iid=2217

2 Intimate Violence. 2008. Crime Characteristics, Bureau of Justice Statistics. Retrieved on February 15, 2010, from http://bjs.ojp.usdoj.gov/index.cfm?ty=pbdetail&iid=2020

3 Officers Killed. 2008. National Law Enforcement Officers Memorial Fund, Inc. Retrieved on January 16, 2011, from http://www.nleomf.org/facts/enforcement/

4 National Crime Victimization Survey. 2009. Bureau of Justice Statistics, Office of Justice Programs, U.S. Department of Justice, Retrieved on 1/13/2011 from http://bjs.ojp.usdoj.gov/index.cfm?ty=tp&tid=43

5 Davis, Matt. 2008. The Thick Blue Line. *The Portland Mercury News*. Retrieved on January 24, 2011 from http://www.portlandmercury.com/portland/Content?oid=717700&category=22101

6 Victim's video marks sentencing as Avery gets life with no parole. June 3, 2007. *Associated Press*. Retrieved on March 4, 2011, from http://www.gmtoday.com/news/special_reports/Halbach_murder/avery_trial.asp

7 Minnesota State Legislature from the Council on Crime and Justice, dated September, 2003.
Retrieved on 1/12/2011, from http://www.irpumn.org/uls/resources/projects/aggregate%20report%2092303.pdf

8 Facts on Post Conviction DNA Exonerations. 2010. *The Innocence Project*. Retrieved on January 16, 2011, from http://www.innocenceproject.org/Content/Facts_on_PostConviction_DNA_Exonerations.php

9 Report of the Metro Gang Task Force Review Panel. August 20, 2009. Minnesota Public Radio. Retrieved on February 16, 2011, from http://minnesota.publicradio.org/features/2009/08/20090820_gangstrikeforce.pdf

10 Lonetree, A. & Brandt, S. December 17, 2010. Minneapolis Settles with Police Sergeant over Gang Strike Force suit. StarTribune.com. 2010. December. Retrieved on 12/13/2010, from http://www.startribune.com/local/112110204.html

11 Dean, S. November 30, 2010. Police sergeant's comments of arresting, beating people at Houston Gay Pride Parade investigated. Houston Page One Examiner. Retrieved on February 13, 2010, from http://www.examiner.com/page-one-in-houston/police-sergeant-s-comments-of-arresting-beating-people-at-houston-gay-pride-parade-investigated.

12 Fitzgerald, R. April 1, 2007. 89 Whistleblowers Feel Vindicated. Sun Herald.com. Retrieved on February 15, 2011, from http://www.waynewoodall.com/Article/ANDREAGIBBS-1.pdf

13 Walsh. J. November, 2010. Former Mpls. Cop Found Not Guilty of Using Unreasonable Force. StarTribune.com. Retrieved on 12/13/2010, from http://www.startribune.com/local/108754689.html

14 Title 42 USC Section 1983. Office of the Law Revision Counsel, U.S. House of Representatives. Retrieved March 5, 2011, from http://uscode.house.gov/uscode-cgi/fastweb.exe?getdoc+uscview+t41t42+3019+0++%28%29%20%20AND%20%28%2842%29%20ADJ%20USC%29%3ACITE%20AND%20%28USC%20w%2F10%20%281983%29%29%3ACITE%20%20%20%20%20%20%20%20%20

15 Title 18 USC Section 242.Office of the Law Revision Counsel, U.S. House of Representatives.

    Retrieved on March 5, 2011, from http://uscode.house.gov/uscode-cgi/fastweb.exe?getdoc+uscview+t17t20+281+0++%28%20%29%20%20AND%20%28%2818%29%20ADJ%20USC%29%3ACITE%20AND%20%28USC%20w%2F10%20%28242%29%29%3ACITE%20%20%20%20%20%20%20%20%20

16 United States Department of Justice Press Release. February 24, 2009. Three Former Atlanta Police Officers Sentenced to Federal Prison in Fatal Shooting of Elderly Atlanta Woman. Defendants Pleaded Guilty to Conspiracy to Violate Civil Rights Resulting in the Death of 92-Year Old Atlanta Resident Kathryn Johnston. Public Affairs Release. Retrieved on March 4, 2011 from http://atlanta.fbi.gov/dojpressrel/pressrel09/at022409.htm

17 United States Department of Justice Press Release. September 29, 2010. Two Former Birmingham Police Officers Indicted for Civil Rights Violations. Public Affairs Release. Retrieved on March 4, 2011 from http://birmingham.fbi.gov/dojpressrel/pressrel10/bh092910.htm

18 United States Department of Justice. Dec 11, 2007. Three Former Milwaukee Police Officers Sentenced on Civil Rights-related Charges. Reported in civilrightslawfirms.com.

    Retrieved on March 4, 2001, from http://www.civilrightslawfirms.com/national-content.cfm/Article/110301/Three-Former-Milwaukee-Police-Officers.html

19 Department of Justice Press Release. August 20, 2010. Natchez, Mississippi Police Officers Indicted for Civil Rights Offenses, Conspiracy to Commit Identity Theft and Fraud, and False Statements. Public Affairs Release. Retrieved on March 4, 2011, from http://jackson.fbi.gov/dojpressrel/pressrel10/ja082010.htm

GLOSSARY

10 Fatal Errors that have killed experienced lawmen:

1. Your attitude
If you fail to keep your mind on the job while on patrol or you carry problems from home into the field, you will start to make errors. It can cost you or other fellow officers their lives. Are you wearing your bullet-resistant armor? It could save your life.

2. Tombstone courage
No one doubts that you are courageous. But in any situation where time allows ,wait for the backup. There are few instances where alone, unaided, you should try to make a dangerous
apprehension.

3. Not enough rest
To do your job you must be alert. Being sleepy or asleep on the job is not only against regulations, but you endanger yourself, the community, and all your fellow officers.

4. Taking a bad position
Never let anyone you are questioning or about to stop get in a better position than you and your vehicle. There is no such thing as a routine call or stop. They are all "unknown risk" calls or stops.

5. Danger signs
As a lawman you will get to recognize danger signs. Movements, strange cars, warnings that should alert you to watch your step and approach with caution. Know your beat and your community—and watch for what is out of place.

6. Failure to watch hands of a suspect
Is he or she reaching for a weapon or getting ready to strike you? Where else can a potential killer strike but from his or her hands?

7. Relaxing too soon
The rut of false alarms that are accidentally set off. Walking in and asking if the place is being held up. Observe the activity. Never take any call as routine, or just another false alarm. It's your life on the line.

8. Improper use or no handcuffs
Once you have made an arrest, handcuff the prisoner and do it properly. See that the hands that can kill are safely cuffed.

9. No search or poor search
There are so many places to hide weapons that your failure to search is a crime against fellow officers. Many criminals carry several weapons and are able and prepared to use them against you.

10. Dirty or inoperative weapon
Is your firearm clean? Will it fire? How about the ammo? When did you last fire so that you can hit a target in combat conditions? What's the sense of carrying any firearm that may not work?
(The Virginia Coalition of Police and Deputy Sheriffs http://www.virginia-cops.org/Articles/Fatal/10Errors.htm)

30+ lbs of equipment:
A street cop will carry anywhere from 20 to 40 pounds of equipment including: 1) body armor, 2) duty weapon, 3) additional ammunition, 4) high intensity flashlight, 5) baton, 6) taser, 7) chemical aerosol, 8) handcuffs, 1 or 2 pair, 9) leather belt and gun belt, 10) leather carriers for all equipment, 11) key ring with assorted keys, 12) backup weapon, this can be anything from a single shot .22 derringer to a .45-caliber semi-auto handgun,
13) high-top leather boots with puncture proof soles, 14) portable radio, 15) cell phone, 16) in winter add parka, gloves, and insulated winter boots.

.45 Cal Thompson:
This is the old two-handed "Tommy Gun" you see in the movies about Al Capone. It is still possible to buy this weapon in a semi-automatic. It shoots a .45-cal bullet and uses high-capacity magazines. The particular weapon we recovered was allegedly used in an execution murder. It had several notches carved into the stock. It has been replaced for the most part by smaller and more accurate 9 mm automatic weapons.

Academy way:
The academy way is usually a derogatory term used by street cops to describe the touchy-feely mandated courses in the academy. Older street cops, who don't bother to keep up on their professional training or legal updates, will use the term in a derogatory manner to describe how new cops try to apply some of the best practices they learned in the academy.

GLOSSARY

Body armor:
Body armor is a bullet-resistant vest or other covering that
protects the officer from most handgun and shotgun projectiles. High-quality
body armor will sustain multiple hits. Blunt trauma from the impact of the
bullet still causes injury to the person shot; the larger the caliber, the greater
the injury. On average, 25 percent of the officers killed by gunfire are wearing vests at the time they are shot.

Bullet-resistant shield:
This is a hand-held shield that is used when entering a building where extra
protection is required as a search is conducted. It weighs about 35 pounds.
The point officer will carry this shield with one arm and their handgun in
their other hand.

Cop:
1) British slang for copper started because of the copper buttons on the Bob-
   bies' uniforms
2) to cop an Attitude
3) Constable On Patrol
4) a slang verb that meant capture

Deliberate indifference:
This was the finding in the civil trial of Mike Sauro where the jury found the
city liable for "maintaining a custom of deliberate indifference to complaints
about excessive force in the department."

Fake Rolex watch:
The theft of any item from a person is a felony in Minnesota and many
other states. The value of the item is irrelevant. We used fake watches and
other fake jewelry in many of our decoy cases.

FBI/SWAT:
For a few years the Minneapolis FBI SWAT team was comprised of Minneapolis Police officers and FBI agents.

Front-end loader:
Heavy construction equipment used to move dirt or debris. With the front
bucket raised, the driver would move forward and could take out the whole
corner of a house in one pass. It was used to gain entry in several barricaded
drug houses in Minneapolis. Eventually someone realized the risk created

by this type of entry and it is now considered for use only in extreme circumstances.

FTO/Field Training Program:
Most police departments have a mandatory Field Training Program that the new officer must successfully pass. It is the "on the job training" portion of learning to be a cop. It is also a time for screening out those who may do well in the academic portion of the training but are unable to apply their knowledge to rapidly evolving situations. Unfortunately, this probably applies to at least 15 percent of the applicants that complete the academic portion. My personal belief is that we could greatly improve the training on the academic and skills end and improve our overall success in the field training program. The FTO is the Field Training Officer is selected to train new cops. Depending on the department, they may be volunteers, or not. The quality of any new cop is directly related to the quality of their field training officer.

High-risk warrants:
A warrant of this type means you do not have to knock, you will usually make a forced entry, and you expect the occupants are armed. It is often used in crack/cocaine warrants. Every crack house has a gun in it. If they didn't, they would be ripped off by their competitors as soon as they set up operations.

Minneapolis Police Emergency Response Unit:
The Minneapolis Police SWAT team. SWAT was considered politically incorrect because of the reputation of the Los Angeles SWAT teams.

Packaged-for-sale crack cocaine:
When crack is ready for sale, it is wrapped in small plastic bundles (rocks) that sell for about $20 each, depending on what the market will bear.

Personal use:
Dealers who carry a small amount will go to court and claim that the crack they were carrying was for personal use and not for sale. Often, they will get away with it.

Ram:
The ram is used to knock down doors or other barricades. Depending on the use, the "hand held" model can weigh up to 140 pounds and requires two

officers to swing it, although I have seen a single officer operate a 120-pound ram with great effectiveness.

Reconnaissance:
Reconnaissance, recon, of a site includes address, type of structure, whether the door you are entering swings in or out (this can be critical), other doors and windows, any barricades, dogs in yard or building, surrounding buildings, number of people inside, weapons that may be in the building, prior arrests or warrants at the address, and escape routes. For the team making the entry, it includes radio communications, tools needed to gain entry, number of officers needed, route to use going in, time of day to do warrant, number of people you expect to encounter, whether there are children present, and about a dozen other issues that each team member must be ready to deal with.

REFERENCES

Adams, Jim. 2004. State Trooper suspended for 30 days. *Minneapolis Star Tribune*. Retrieved on March 19, 2004, from http://www.startribune.com

Agathocieous, Alexis. 1998. Prosecuting Police Misconduct: Reflections on the Role of the U.S. Civil Rights Division. Vera Institute of Justice, New York. Retrieved from http://www.vera.org

Austin City Connection. April 2, 2001. Statement Concerning Verdict In Samuel Ramirez Trial. Retrieved on December 2, 2003, from http://www.ci.austin.tx.us/police/copverdict 0401.htm

Avery, Steven. Victim sends apology to Steven Avery. The Associated Press. *Milwaukee Herald Times*. Retrieved on April 8, 2004, from http://www.wisinfo.com/heraldtimes/news/archive/local_12399159.shtml

Chanen, David. July 1, 1998. Three indicted in '96 slaying of Byron Phillips. *Minneapolis Star Tribune*. Retrieved on April 6, 2004, from http://www.startribune.com

Crime and Victims Statistics. 2002. U.S. Department of Justice, Office of Justice Programs, Bureau of Justice Statistics. Retrieved on April 12, 2004, from http://www.ojp.usdoj.gov/bjs/cvictgen.htm

Cummins, Jeanine. 2004. *A Rip in Heaven.* Penguin: New York.

Department of Medical Entomology. 2003. Body Lice. Retrieved on January 15, 2004, from http://medent.usydedu.au/fact/bodylice.html

Diaz, Kevin. June 28, 1986. 10 officers suspended in police decoy case. *Minneapolis Star Tribune*. Retrieved on December 4, 2003, from http://nl.newsbank.com/nl-search/we/Archives?p_action=doc&p_docid=oefe498eF3199

Diaz, Kevin. March 22, 1986. Decoy Unit Evidence Rejected. *Minneapolis Star Tribune*. Retrieved on December 4, 2003, from http://nl.newsbank.com/nl-search/we/Archives?p_action=doc&pdocid=odfd4974e6eco

Drug Policy Alliance. 2003. Drugs, Police & the Law. Police Corruption. Retrieved on December 1, 2003, from http://www.drugpolicy.org/law/police/

Electronic Telegraph. 1998. The Shameful Truth about Police Corruption. Retrieved on December 14, 2003, from http://www.telegraph.co.uk/

Freedom to Care. 1999. Is ethical policing possible? Retrieved on December 14, 2003, from http://www.freedomtocare.org/contents.htm#police

Fahrenthold, David A. October 26, 2003. Arrested Police a Worry in D.C., Washington Post Company. Retrieved on December 4, 2003, from http://studentvoices.org/news/index/.php3?NewsID=7709

Federal Bureau of Investigation. 2002. Law Enforcement Officers Killed and Assaulted.Retreived on April 12, 2004, from http://www.fbi.gov/ucr /ucr.htm

Ferrell, Craig E. November 2003. Code of Silence: Fact or Fiction. *The Police Chief.*

Frankl, Viktor E. 1963. *Man's Search for Meaning.* Simon and Schuster: New York.

Gamma Globulin. Retrieved on January 15, 2004 from http://www.slider.com/Enc/G/Ga/Gammaglo.htm

Gold, Scott. August 23, 2003. 35 Are Pardoned in Texas Drug Case Saturday. *Los Angeles Times.* Retrieved on April 14, 2004, from http://www.november.org/stayinfo/breaking/Tulia8-03.html

Goleman, Daniel.1995. *Emotional Intelligence.* Bantam Books: New York.

——— 1998. *Working with Emotional Intelligence.* Bantam Books: New York.

Grant, Mary Lee. March 23, 2004. Residents Air Police Concerns. Retrieved on April 4, 2004, from http://HoustonChronicle.com

Harris, Eldon. November 10, 2003. Cop Crimes. Retrieved on April 4, 2004, from http://www.Copcrimes.com.

Hennepin County Office of Planning and Development. 2000. African-American Men Project Final Report. Minneapolis, Minnesota. Retrieved on April 14, 2004, from http://www.co.hennepin.mn.us/vgn/portal /internet/hcdetailmaster/0,2300,1273_1716_100433679,00.html

Sources quoted in African American Men Project Final Report.

42 The disparities between Minneapolis and its suburbs are not the result of natural forces.

They arose during the 1940s and 1950s as by-products of both legal and de facto segregation.

This segregation continued well into the 1960s and 1970s—both legally, through white flight, restrictive covenants, mortgage redlining, exclusionary zoning, and federal housing and transportation policy— and illegally, through the real estate practice of steering white home buyers toward white neighborhoods and black home buyers toward black (i.e., generally poor) ones.

There is some evidence that this last practice continued well into the 1990s, and may still be with us. As suburban sprawl grew, and many whites and middle-class blacks moved from Minneapolis to the suburbs, poverty became more and more concentrated in the city's five poorest communities. This flight of many middle-class people of all races to the suburbs has helped to deepen the very disparities that these people hoped to leave behind. For a detailed treatment of this subject on a national level, see Douglas Massey and Nancy Denton's book *American Apartheid* (Harvard University Press, 1994).

43 This study, "How African American Men Are Faring in 11 U.S. Cities," is included in the Research Compendium published simultaneously with this report. Data used in this study were drawn from a variety of sources: "1998 Current Population Survey," U.S. Department of Education Common Core of Data, National Center for Education Studies (1998 data), 1999 local area unemployment statistics, "Corrections Populations in 1996" and the National Vital Statistics System.

44 Office of Planning and Development staff also examined relevant data from three other sources:

1) "Metropolitan Racial and Ethnic Change—Census 2000," a 2001 study produced by the Lewis Mumford Center for Comparative Urban and Regional Research; 2) 1988–95 data on Minnesota and the Minneapolis/St. Paul Metropolitan Statistical Area (MSA) from the U.S. Department of Labor's Bureau of Statistics (this data appeared in the African American Men Project Preliminary Report); and 3) 1990-97 data on Hennepin County from the Equal Employment Opportunity Commission (which also appeared in the African American Men Project Preliminary Report).

45 Incarceration rates for adult males in Minnesota in 1996 were 156 per 100,000 whites, 4,169 per 100,000 African Americans. Source: "Corrections Populations in 1996." Statistics are for the latest year for which sufficient data are available.

46 Death rates in Minnesota in 1995–97 were 401.1 for non-Hispanic whites, 675.7 for blacks.

Source: National Vital Statistics System. Statistics are for the latest years for which sufficient data are available.

47 Source: Department of Education Common Core of Data, 1997 data. School districts for only 6 of the 11 cities studied were compared: Minneapolis, Cleveland, Portland, St. Louis, San Diego, and Atlanta City/Fulton County.

48 Source: National Center for Education Statistics, 1998 data. It should also be noted that, among all 11 major American metropolitan areas, there is not one in which young African American men are doing as well (or even nearly as well) as their white counterparts.

Houston Police Department Badge lost some of its luster recently. Retrieved on April 4, 2004, from Click2Houston.com

Human Rights Watch. 1998. Shielded from Justice: Police Brutality and Accountability: Minneapolis: Incidents. Retrieved on December 1, 2003, from http://www.hrw.org/reports98/police/uspo84.htm

Human Rights Watch. 2000. United States—Punishment and Prejudice: Racial Disparities in the War on Drugs. Retrieved on September 16, 2002, from http://www.hrw.org/reports/2000/usa/Rcedrg00-01.htm

Human Rights Watch. Shielded from Justice: Police Brutality and Accountability in the United States. Retrieved on July 22, 2004, from http://www.hrw.org/reports98/police/uspo86.htm

Hunt, G,. ed. 1998. Is ethical policing possible? *Freedom to Care.* Cheltenham, England.

Hvass, Sheryl R. 2001. 2001 Commissioner's Report. The State of the Prison Population. Minnesota Department of Corrections. St. Paul, Minnesota.

Imperfect Justice. May 28, 2001. Editorial. *The Washington Post Company.* Retrieved on December 4, 2003, from http://www.truthinjustice.org/gilchrist2.htm

REFERENCES

Intimate Violence. 2002. Crime Characteristics, Bureau of Justice Statistics. Retrieved on April 14, 2004, from http://www.ojp.usdoj.gov/bjs/cvict_c.htm.

Josephson Institute of Ethics, The. http://www.josephsoninstitute.org

Justice Project, The. Campaign for Criminal Justice Reform. Retrieved on January 17, 2004, from http:/justice.policy.net/proactive /newsroom/release.vtml?id=31860

KGO-TV/DT San Francisco. The education of Keith Bratt—continued. Retrieved on January 17, 2004, from http://abclocal.go.com/kgo /news/120903_nw_oakland_riders.html

LAPD Whistleblower Gets Prison Term. upi News. Retrieved on April 14, 2004 from http://www.newmax.com/articles/?a=2000 /2/26/71107

LeDoux, Joseph. 1996.*The Emotional Brain: The Mysterious Underpinnings of Emotional Life.* Simon and Schuster: New York.

MacArthur Justice Center, The. 2000. Man Coerced Into False Confession Files Suit Against Chicago Police. Retrieved on January 17, 2003, from http://macarthur.uchicago.edu/pdf/Bell_pressrelease.pdf

McNamara Collection. Shaffer Library of Drug Policy. Retrieved on July 22, 2004, from http://www.druglibrary.org/schaffer/debate/mcn/mcn9,htm

Meyerhoff, B.G. 1978. *Number Our Days.* Simon and Schuster: New York.

Mollen, Milton. 1994. Commission to Investigate Allegations of Police Corruption and the Anti-Corruption Procedures of the Police Department, Commission Report. New York.

National Law Enforcement Officers Memorial Fund, Inc., Brian Gibson and Jerry Haaf. Retrieved on December 13, 2003, from http://www.nleomf.com/

Quinn, J., J. Duncanson, J. Rankin. August, 16, 2001. RCMP probes Toronto police corruption: Senior Mountie heads inquiries into disgraced drug squad. *Toronto Star.* Retrieved January 14, 2003, from http://www.walnet.org/jane_doe2001/torstar-010816.html

Scorsese, M. and S. Lee, prod. 1995. *Clockers*. 40 Acres and a Mule Film Works. Universal Pictures: USA.

Scott, Sal Saran. Communities United Against Police Brutality. Retrieved on April 8, 2004, from http://www.charityadvantage .com/cuapb/SalSaranScott.asp

Seed, G. and A. Palmer. September 27, 1998. Police Corruption in UK 'at Third World levels.' *UK Telegraph*. Retrieved on December 1, 2003, from http://www.telegraph.co.uk/html

Silvester, John. February 17, 2003. Police face criminal charges. *The Age*. Retrieved on December 1, 2003, from http://www.theage .com.au /articles/2003/02/16/1045330468981.html

Stuckey, T. November 1, 2003. Wrongfully Convicted Man Pardoned: Free after serving 27 years on Murder Charge. AP. Retrieved on November 1, 2003, from http://aolsvc.news.aol.com/news/article.adp ?id=20031101012309990001

Texas Department of Health, Infectious Disease Epidemiology and Surveillance Division, Hepatitis C. http://www.TDH.state.tx.us

Thompson, A.C. August 22, 2001. How to blow a police corruption case: Why the prosecution of the Oakland "Riders" is likely to fail. *San Francisco Bay Guardian*. Retrieved on December 1, 2003, from http://www. sfbg.com/News/35/47/47riders.html

Truth in Justice. Recent Cases. Retrieved on January 16, 2003, from http:// www.truthinjustice.org/index.htm

United States Department of Justice. January 5, 2000. Former West New York Police Chief Sentenced to 49 Months in Prison. Public Affairs Release. Retrieved on December 2, 2003, from http://www.usdoj.gov/usao/nj /publicaffairs/releases/wn0105_r.htm

United States General Accounting Office. 1998. Report to the Honorable Charles B. Rangel, House of Representatives. Information on Drug-Related Police Corruption. gao Publication No. GAO/GGD-98-111. Washington, DC.

University of Sydney, Australia, Dept. of Medical Entomology. Retrieved on July 18, 2004, from http://medent.usyd.edu.au/FACT/BodyLice.html

REFERENCES

Weisbrud, D., R. Greenspan, E.E. Hamilton, H. Williams, and K.A. Bryant. 2000. Police Attitudes Toward Abuse of Authority: Findings From a National Study. NCJ Publication No. 181312. National Institute of Justice: Research in Brief, Washington, DC.

ADDITIONAL READINGS AND RESOURCES

I do not necessarily endorse any of these sites except as noted.

9/11 Digital Archive—http://www.911digitalarchive.org/

African American Links (excellent site for history lessons)—http://blackquest.com/link.htm

African American Men Project—http://www.co.hennepin.mn.us/vgn/portal/internet/hcdetailmaster/0,2300,1273_1716_100433679,00.html

Bigots with Badges—http://www.bwbadge.com/

Black History Pages: Lynchingshttp://blackhistorypages.com/Lynching/

Bureau of Justice Statistics Homepage—http://www.ojp.usdoj.gov/bjs/

Calibre Press (Your best source of police training and updates)—http://www.calibrepress.com/home/login.html

Centre for the Study of Violence and Reconciliation Tackling Police Corruption in South Africa —http://www.csvr.org.za/papers/papoli14.htm

Center for Public Integrity, The— http://www.publicintegrity.org/default.aspx

Consequences of the Police State, The—http://www.worldfreeinternet.net/news/nws131.htm

Cops and Police Stories—http://www.powells.com/subsection/CrimeCopsandPoliceStories.4.html

cops Office Police Training Officer Manual—http://www.cops.usdoj.gov/Default.asp?Item=971

Corruption in England and Wales: An assessment of current evidence Home Office Online Report—
http://www.homeoffice.gov.uk/rds/pdfs2/rdsolr1103.pdf

Corruption in West Vancouver Police Department—
http://www.geocities.com/CapitolHill/Senate/3853/

Crime, Corruption, and Terrorism in the Former ussr, Eastern Europe, and the Middle East—http://www.rferl.org/reports/corruptionwatch/

Criminal Justice Resources http://www.lib.msu.edu/harris23/crimjust/index.htm

Drug Policy Alliance, The—http://www.drugpolicy.org/law/police/

Ethics in Policing—http://www.freedomtocare.org/contents.htm#police

FBI Law Enforcement Bulletin (every cop should subscribe)—http://www.fbi.gov/publications/leb/leb.htm

Federal Bureau of Investigation Uniform Crime Reports—http://www.fbi.ov/ucr/ucr.htm

Greensboro Sitins, The—http://www.sitins.com/

Hoser Files, The—http://www.smuggled.com/vrb1.htm

IN THE NEWS!!!—http://www.leoaffairs.com/left_frame_files/in_the_news.htm

Incarceration and Race—The Human Rights Watch—http://www.hrw.org/reports/2000/usa/Rcedrg0001.htm#P149_24292

Index of Native American Resources on the Internet—
http://www.hanksville.org/NAresources/

Josephson Institute of Ethics, The (*The best site on web for ethics training. Michael Josephson pulls no punches!*)—
http://www.josephsoninstitute.org/

Law Enforcement Memorial Directory—
http://www.officer.com/memorial.htm

Law Enforcement Sites on the Web—http://www.ih2000.net/ira/ira.htm

mexico: Massive Corruption in Police. April 13, 2004: The Mexican state of Morelos suspended all (522) of the detectives on its state police force— http://strategypage.com/fyeo/qndguide/default.asp? target=mexico.htm

National Center for Women and Policing (excellent source)—http://www. womenandpolicing.org/publications.asp

National Institute of Justice Publications— http://nij.ncjrs.org/publications/

National Law Enforcement Officers Memorial Fund—http://www.nleomf. com/FallenOfficers/LineofDuty/helping.html

National Law Enforcement Officers Tributes To Fallen Officers—http:// www.nleomf.com/FallenOfficers/LineofDuty/tributes.html

New Zealand undercover police officers broke their silence and alleged perjury and corruption—http://www.norml.org.nz/article402.html

November Coalition, The— http://www.november.org/stayinfo/breaking/Tulia8-03.html

Orangeburg Massacre— http://www.afroamhistory.about.com/cs/civilrights/a /orangeburg.htm

Police Links—Web Links for Researchers— http://www.freedomtocare.org/page122.htm

Source for Law Enforcement and Police, The—http://www.officer.com/

The Virgin Islands. Crime investigations—and a former police academy instructor . . . testify in a notorious corruption case—http://www.virginislandsdailynews.com/index.pl/article_home?id=4799839

United States Holocaust Memorial Museum—http://www.ushmm.org/

Vera Institute of Justice—Advancing Justice through Innovation—http:// www.vera.org/

WHISTLEBLOWER ARTICLES

$6 Million to Be Paid in 9 Police Suits. A city attorney warned that juries could award huge damages if the whistle-blower cases— http://www.pipeline.com/~rgibson/racistlapd.html

A Whistleblower Feels the Heat. New Haven's chief investigates the cop who spoke . . . Keith Wortz learned this week what happens to cops who expose corruption—http://www.newhavenadvocate.com /gbase/News/content.html?oid=oid:35358

Terry Lane talks to a leading criminologist and to a former drug squad officer turned whistleblower about the relationship between cops and drugs—http://www.abc.net.au/rn/talks/natint/stories /s905165.htm

Whistleblower goes to Prison. . . . An incredible, long series on abusive cops in the Seattle Post-Intelligence Washington Post series on false confessions Ontario—http://www.injusticebusters.com/04/Erickson _Steve.htm

LAPD Whistleblower Gets Prison Term. . . . beyond the exoneration of innocent people, that what he wants most now is ". . . to remind the greenest rookie cops that they . . . —http://www.newsmax.com/articles /?a=2000/2/26/71107

Good cops need maximum help to minimize the incidence of bad cops. The nsw Government must ensure that whistleblower protection legislation fully protects—http://www.andrewmurray.democrats.org.au /documents/268/PoliceCorruption-OpEd.pdf

A Whistleblower Feels the Heat (News) Keith Wortz learned this week what happens to cops who expose corruption—they become targets themselves. Paul Bass—http://www.newhavenadvocate.com/gbase /archives/index?date=oid:35359

He's a whistleblower. "I've been called many things," he says. . . . We, as cops, have a responsibility to see people treated right, and we abuse—http://www.citybeat.com/2001-06-28/negrotour.shtml

More cops are willing to break the code of silence. In a dark alley with a robbery in progress, they have few other people to rely on, other than cops. . . . He filed suit under the city's whistleblower law last year . . . http://search.csmonitor.com/durable/1997/08/20/us/us.2.html

INDEX

abusive language 126, 134
adrenaline 14, 15, 22, 23, 24, 42, 43, 44, 52, 83, 84, 130
African American Men Project Final Report 8, 169
America's Plague of Bad Cops 149
amygdala hijack 26, 30, 43
an amoral perversion of the truth xii, xiii
attitude 83, 131, 142, 144, 145, 156, 159, 162
Avery, Steven 92-94, 167

backup officers 17, 23, 114
bad apples xi
bad decisions xiii, 131
baggie of crack cocaine 89-90
blood borne pathogens 54
blue xii, 26, 33
body armor 4, 22, 84, 88, 161, 162
Bouza, Tony 98
burglary committed by cops 37

Civilian Review 19, 20, 46
Clockers 80, 172
Code of Silence xi, xii, xiii, 3, 4, 6, 13, 25, 26, 30, 33, 35, 38, 45, 46, 47, 55, 67, 71, 72, 74, 81, 82, 100, 101, 107, 109, 111, 116, 117, 123, 131, 132, 140, 147, 148, 150, 156, 168, 177
communication 142-149
community trust 7, 101
community's expectations 133
convict and incarcerate xi, 11, 67, 79, 90, 96, 135, 136
courage 138, 159

cover for each other v, 19
crack dealers 72, 78, 80, 84, 110
creative report writing xii, 6, 47, 69, 96

Dad 1-2, 103
dark side 25
deadly force 31, 126
deliberate indifference 71, 162
derogatory terms 130
Dershowitz, Alan M. 90
Don and Ted 128
drug addiction 86
drug dealers xii, 72, 77, 78, 79, 86, 88, 99, 151

Emergency Response Unit 44, 83, 164
ethical dilemmas 13
ethical police conduct 5
ethics 11, 12, 25, 72, 109, 153, 171, 174, 175
excessive force 14, 17, 18, 45, 52, 59, 66, 73, 97, 99, 100, 105, 115, 126, 129, 133, 134, 162

false alarm 36, 160
family of cops 1
FBI 5, 63, 87, 102, 106
fear system 27, 28
female deputy 141
Field Training 28, 35, 47, 70, 107, 108, 109, 117, 118, 140, 163
first cop to tell the truth 19

gamma globulin 54, 168
Gardner, Howard 137
Gibson, Brian 4, 172

Gilchrist, Joyce 106
good cops xi, 3, 6, 19, 20, 33, 47, 79,
  100, 101, 131, 149, 176
gut reaction 26, 27, 29, 115

Haaf, Jerry 5, 172
Hennepin County 7-10, 44, 126, 134,
  135, 168, 170
hepatitis 54, 58, 60, 172
high-capacity firearms 4
high-risk warrant service 83
HIV 54, 58, 60

I'm not playing 35, 38, 41, 68
Internal Affairs 18, 19, 20, 46, 58, 63,
  69, 70, 71, 72, 74, 97, 99, 125

Josephson Institute of Ethics 25, 171,
  175
jump out 80
justice system, injury to 12

Leading Minds: An Anatomy of
  Leadership 137
LeDoux, Joseph 27

macho man 143-144
mandate 12
McNamara, Robert 149
Minneapolis cop 33
Minneapolis Urban League 100
Myerhoff, Barbara 121

National Institute of Justice 4, 173, 175
National Law Enforcement Officers
  Memorial Fund 4, 21, 172, 175
Number Our Days 121, 171

officer needs help 13-14, 49

Olson, Mike 153
Orangeburg Massacre 103, 175

Parent, Michael Ray 110
Phillips, Byron 44, 167
pockets of corruption xi
positive changes 45
poverty 9, 78, 127, 169
prisoner 17, 59-63, 93, 120, 151, 160
proactive supervision 148
prostitute 39-41
protect and serve xi, 12, 90, 96, 138, 153

reach down deep 22
reconnaissance 83, 87, 164
recruits xi, 21, 23, 28, 46-47, 68, 70, 71,
  107, 118, 140-144
Repeat Offender Program 115, 126
ride-alongs 47, 68
ripple effect 105, 136
rite of passage 38
Robbery/Decoy Unit 112, 126
rookie 35, 38, 50-52, 55-67, 108, 118, 176

save their lives 22
Scott, Sal Saran 97
service to others 2
sixth sense 27-28
snitch 34, 39-41, 66, 70
snitched 33-34, 65
Soulis, Pete 22
Sudduth, Gary 100

test of our character 25
testi-lying xii
training xiii, 1, 11, 21-24, 28, 30, 31, 34,
  35, 38, 45, 46, 47, 50, 55, 56, 57, 68, 70,
  71, 107, 108, 109, 117, 118, 124, 139,
  140-148, 152, 161, 163, 173, 174, 175

truth xii, xiii, 7, 19, 20, 24, 31, 41, 62, 63, 64-67, 72, 83, 92-94, 105, 117, 138, 168, 172

undercover 77, 80, 85, 145, 155, 175
unethical behavior 6, 152
University of Minnesota's Institute on Race and Poverty 9
use of force 14, 51, 52, 55, 56, 58, 67, 103, 108, 119, 134

Vera Institute of Justice 102, 167, 176
violent domestic 14

war on drugs 7, 77-78, 107
will to live 21
Working with Emotional Intelligence 138, 168

you can be killed 15

MIKE QUINN

It is no wonder that Mike Quinn can think like a crook and still act like a cop. He's been in law enforcement for 25 years, 23 ½ of those with the Minneapolis Police Department and 18 months with the Minnesota Police Corps where he oversaw the design and development of the federally sponsored Police Corps Academy. During his tenure with the Force, Mike worked in some of the toughest and highest-profile units, serving over 300 high-risk warrants without a critical incident, conducting successful raids on armed and dangerous suspects, and diligently investigating allegations of internal criminal and departmental violations. He is the recipient of numerous awards, including departmental Commendations, Awards of Merit, and a Unit Citation, an Outstanding Service Award from the FBI, a Leadership award from the Urban League, two Meritorious Masts from the United States Marine Corps, and the Lifetime Achievement in Law Enforcement Training award from the Association of Training of Officers of Minnesota.

He is an acknowledged contributor to *The Tactical Edge* by Calibre Press and he regularly teaches and has testified as an expert witness on such topics as Self Defense for Civilians, Search and Seizure, Firearms, Rappelling, Defensive Tactics, Pressure Point Control Tactics, Deadly Force, Chemical Agents, High Risk Warrants, and SWAT Tactics.

A lifelong resident of Minneapolis, Mike lives with his wife of 40-plus years, with whom he shares a love for distance running, mountain biking, and the great outdoors.

Mike's success in law enforcement is reflected in the passion and commitment he brings to being an ethical cop. *Walking with the Devil* is another example of this commitment.